ALTERED ART

ALTERED ART

TECHNIQUES FOR CREATING ALTERED BOOKS, BOXES, CARDS & MORE

Terry Taylor

LARK BOOKS

A Division of
Sterling Publishing Co., Inc.
New York

Library of Congress Cataloging-in-Publication Data

Taylor, Terry, 1952-
  Altered art : techniques for creating altered books, boxes, cards & more /
Terry Taylor.
    p. cm.
  Includes index.
  ISBN 1-57990-550-1 (hardcover)
 1. Handicraft. I. Title.
TT857.T39 2004
745.5--dc22

                                                      2004005313

10 9 8 7

Published by Lark Books, a division of
Sterling Publishing Co., Inc.
387 Park Avenue South, New York 10016

© 2004, Lark Books

Distributed in Canada by Sterling Publishing,
c/o Canadian Manda Group, 165 Dufferin Street
Toronto, Ontario, Canada M6K 3H6

Distributed in the United Kingdom by GMC Distribution Services,
Castle Place, 166 High Street, Lewes, East Sussex, England BN7 1XU

Distributed in Australia by Capricorn Link (Australia) Pty Ltd.,
P.O. Box 704, Windsor, NSW 2756 Australia

If you have questions or comments about this book, please contact:
Lark Books, 67 Broadway, Asheville, NC 28801, (828) 253-0467

Manufactured in China

All rights reserved

ISBN 13: 978-1-57990-550-7
ISBN 10: 1-57990-550-1

For information about custom editions, special sales, premium and
corporate purchases, please contact Sterling Special Sales Department
at 800-805-5489 or specialsales@sterlingpub.com.

ART DIRECTOR: Kristi Pfeffer

COVER DESIGNER: Barbara Zaretsky

EDITORIAL ASSISTANCE: Delores Gosnell, Jeff Hamilton,
Rosemary Kast, Rebecca Guthrie, Nathalie Mornu

ASSOCIATE ART DIRECTORS: Lance Wille, Shannon Yokeley

EDITORIAL INTERNS: Meghan McGuire, Ryan Sniatecki

ART INTERNS: Melanie Cooper, Jason Thompson

PHOTOGRAPHY: Martin Fox Photography (Martin Fox and
Sallye Fox) and Blackbox Photography (Steve Mann)

COVER IMAGES Clockwise from top left: Chris Young,
Tracy Roos, Jean Tomaso Moore, Lina Trudeau Olson

FRONT FLAP Terry Taylor

BACK COVER Clockwise from top left: Nicole Tuggle,
Carol Owen, Deborah Hayner

BACK FLAP Lynn Whipple

SPINE Patricia Chapman

TITLE PAGE From left to right:
DAYLE DOROSHOW, *Take Flight*, 2003
Driftwood, polmer clay, wire, carving, millefiore canework,
feathers, 16 x 4 x 4 in. (40.6 x 10.2 x 10.2 cm)
Photo by Don Felton

MADONNA C. PHILLIPS, *Rosebud*, 2003
Wood box, acrylic paint, collage on mirror glass, oil paint,
shoe, 30 x 15 x 3 in. (76.2 x 38.1 x 7.6 cm)
Photo by Cheryl Gottschall

LYNN WHIPPLE, *Fine Young Man*, 2002
Mixed media assemblage, 13 x 20 in. (33 x 50.8 cm)
Photo by Randall Smith

JUDITH HOYT, *Figure with Circles*, 2003
Found metal, wood, oil paint, 22 x 8 x ¾ in.
(55.8 x 20.3 x 1.9 cm)
Photo by John Lenz

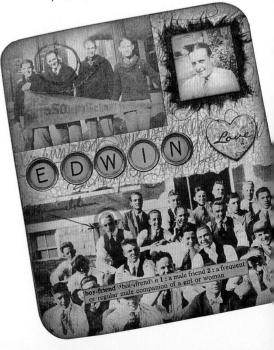

Contents

Introduction

But how does one know what a certain object will tell another?

Joseph Cornell

TERRY TAYLOR, *Angel*, 2001
Sardine can lid, milagros, Red Cross
button, tin, sterling bezel and rivets,
2¾ x 5½ in. (7 x 14 cm)
Collection of Greta Byrd
Photo by Keith Wright

I can pinpoint the time—the week of December 15, 1967—when I became transfixed with the idea of using ordinary objects to create art, even though it would be some 20 years before I actually did so. In that week's issue of *Life* magazine, after reading about the first human heart transplant and ruffles returning to women's fashion, I turned to the first of nine full-color pages of intriguing boxes by someone named Joseph Cornell. (Color was unusual in those distant days; typically only the advertisements were printed in color.)

Why did his arrangement of objects in a handmade box—a fragment of a white clay pipe, silver bangles suspended from a metal rod, cordial glasses holding blue cat's-eye marbles, and a textbook illustration of the solar system—both puzzle and captivate me? The box and its contents didn't fit into any definition of art I knew—it wasn't drawing, oil painting, or marble sculpture—and I didn't have words to describe it.

Later, I would become familiar with terms such as *collage, assemblage*, and *mixed-media* work. And now, the phrase *altered art* has been added to the list of descriptive terms for creative work that doesn't fit into traditional, fine art modes.

Altered art, simply put, uses an object instead of a canvas to convey a singular, artistic expression. It literally alters preconceived notions and ideas about that object. It challenges a viewer's conventional way of looking at, and thinking about, an object. A doll can become more than a simple toy for play. It can be an evocation of a scarred childhood or a celebration of innocence. A discarded jigsaw puzzle of a Venetian scene can become an unusual repository for personal recollections of young love.

Creating altered art doesn't require that you possess fine art skills such as drawing, painting, or sculpting. (But, as they say: If you have them, use them!) It employs both two- and three-dimensional objects as surfaces—and as working materials—for creative expression. It calls on elements of collage and assemblage as well as simple-to-master crafting techniques. This range of materials and approaches is one of the things that makes altered art appealing to such a wide variety of people.

Altered Art will introduce you to basic how-to information that you'll need to start creating your own altered art using books, boxes, cards, or any other object as a starting point. I invited craft designers, artists, and people who simply enjoy making things to create projects for each chapter. The projects include work that uses various art materials (paint, gold leaf, or metal patinas, for example) and simple craft techniques (such as decoupage, stitchery, and rubber-stamping) to transform commonplace objects into works of art. The pages of a child's board book of abc's can be altered with paint and collage to explore our verbal and visual perceptions of jewelry.

TERRY TAYLOR, *Salvation*, 2000
Hatchet, stenciled lettering, vintage Red Cross
blood donor pin, 5½ x 13 in. (14 x 33 cm)
Photo by Robert Chiarito

A pair of recycled blue jeans can be transformed into a journal celebrating personal discovery.

As you read this book, resist the temptation to simply look at the photograph of a project—"I want to make that!"—and skip to the how-to instructions. It's illuminating to read the artists' comments at the beginning of the project. Each comment reveals something invaluable about how or why the artist was inspired to create the piece. Sometimes a unique object was the inspiration; at other times a personal photograph of grandparents, a memento from debutante days, or even a response to a myth was the springboard for a piece. Using memories, bits of random information, and creating or re-interpreting stories can be the starting points for your own work.

Read on to explore the physical processes used to create each project. Don't be surprised to find that you already know many—if not all—of the simple craft techniques used. If a project was created using a unique process or the artist has a helpful working hint, you'll learn about it so that you can use it in one of your own creations.

And finally, each chapter is illustrated with a sampling of the expressive work created by people from all walks of life—metalworkers, woodworkers, full-time artists, and people who hold down 9 to 5 jobs that have nothing to do with art or craft. What these people have in common is the desire to express themselves through the art they create. They use varied objects from the world around them to create different ways of looking at the world, evoke particular emotions, or question our perceptions and pre-conceived notions. You'll be amazed by the variety of the work.

I use both two- and three-dimensional objects as starting points for the art I create. When I select a vintage form for drying sweaters, a rusted sardine

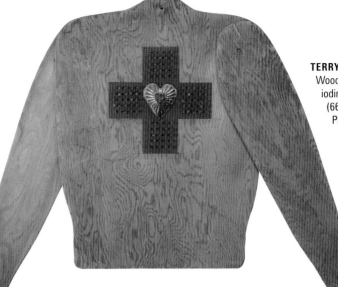

TERRY TAYLOR, *Torso*, 1999
Wood form, nails, pastry mold, iodine, acrylic paint, 26 x 23 in. (66 x 58.4 cm)
Photo by Robert Chiarito

can lid, or a well-used red and white hatchet, each has spoken to me on some level. And then, when I create art with them, references to the human form, ritual objects, or ritual acts are obvious to me. I'm always curious—like Joseph Cornell—what those objects will say to a viewer once I've worked on them—altered them, if you will. It's that opportunity to communicate with a viewer, combined with the urge to create, that compels everyone to make art.

Select an object to alter because it has specific associations for you. A book's pages may remind you of lessons learned (or taught) or the seductive escapism of romantic fiction. If a particular object has meaning for you and you combine it with carefully chosen imagery, text, or other objects, you'll elicit a thoughtful response from a viewer. That's what art—altered or fine—is meant to do.

While reading this book and reveling in the creativity of others, I hope you'll not only be intrigued, but inspired, to create your own altered art as well. Not by imitating the work of others, but by identifying your own personal vision—what you wish to say—and expressing it in the art pieces you create.

Juror's Foreword

Writing these words, I glance out my kitchen window to a world covered by an unexpected snowstorm. The familiar February hues of brown, gray, and evergreen on the surrounding mountains have been temporarily transformed by an icy blanket of pristine crystals that buffer the outside world and make this quaint house feel sweetly cozy in spite of its drafts and chilly floors.

Around my neck is a favorite necklace, fashioned from a crackled, porcelain shard and round, black stones plucked from my beloved Tuckaseegee River. The focal spiral-moon shell, broken by waves on some distant sandy beach, gains new life when drilled, wired, and combined with the other flotsam and jetsam I've gathered on my many journeys. From each of my earlobes dangle round, vintage typewriter keys fashioned into jewelry by a dear friend. They suggest the proper pronunciation for my first name: the number "9" and an "a".

Both of these—my frosty-window view of white mountains and the jewels I wear—reflect the state of alteration, of objects modified. My fat, old, and faded *Webster's New World Dictionary* defines the word alter as "to change, make different, modify." Under this definition are neatly strung such words as alteration, alter ego, and alternator ("dynamo producing alternating current"). This last one brings a smile. I've discovered, in perusing this book's many submissions, that we mixed-media artists are ALL dynamos, creating from scavenged findings new objects of art in eclectic, unpredictable formats that urge us to sit up and take note, to absorb their spontaneous stories and visual narration.

I've been teaching art workshops for three years, and in that brief time have witnessed an incredible surge of interest in the field of assemblage and altered art. Where once I encountered timid students afraid to delve into any given medium, I now happily see thriving artists working feverishly from the beginning of class, then on past closing time, and late into the night. In the sanctuary of their home studios, expressing themselves confidently through bold and vibrant creations, they don't need a teacher's coaxing for the "inner artist" to emerge. I no longer need to remind them that they have the moxie it takes to create an original work of art, as is evident on this book's overflowing gallery pages.

Note that the variety of work in the gallery is by both professionals—teachers and artists whose work is sold in retail galleries—and that of designers who create artwork as a pastime. We have something to

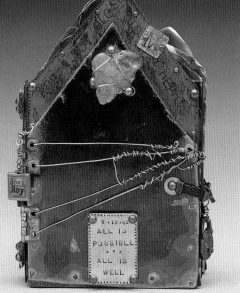

NINA BAGLEY, *Roy's Book*, 2002
Cover: brass, silver, mica, river glass, and vintage lock; inner page pockets: copper mesh, mica, coffee stained paper, and fabric
4 x 6 x 1 in. (10.2 x 15.2 x 2.5 cm)
Photo by Martin Fox

Tucked inside the book is a message: This is for Roy's passage into adulthood—the road has been bumpy but full of beauty.

NINA BAGLEY
Unbreakable, 2004 (detail)
River stone, PMC, lampwork
beads by Mary Jean Martin,
sterling silver wire, mica,
and natural materials
Photo by Martin Fox

NINA BAGLEY, *A Summer Story* (Copper Booklace), 2003
Hammered copper sheet, copper frame, mica pages, copper mesh,
paper, vintage copper chain, beach glass, shell, resin charms.
Photo by Martin Fox

learn from both. When I taught one class a year or so ago, I was both delighted and intimidated to discover that Lynn Whipple (pages 83, 90, 123), whom I'd never met, but whose work I'd admired, had signed up for the class. Lynn's very original whimsical style, her quirky combination of vintage images with contemporary humor, has taught me to loosen up my own solemn approach and to not be afraid of marrying bold color with faded, Victorian sepia images.

Dawn Southworth (page 121) exhibits a solid confidence in simplicity and keen sense of balance and symmetry. Rather than overtly fuss with a lovely but damaged vintage floral painting, she chooses to let the bare beauty of torn pieces shine when sparingly pieced back together. Sparse design speaks just as strongly in Ron Sawyer's work (page 97). He allows the juxtaposition of wings, a lock, and a few succinct words hammered into metal to create an evocative narration of their own.

If I can offer any word of advice, it's an earnest suggestion for each and every student, hobbyist, and professional artist to take himself and his artwork seriously. Honor yourself! Validate your work with organized documentation (if you've seen my disheveled studio, keep laughter to a polite level, please) and clear, high-quality photography.

Too many times during the jurying, unfortunately, a talented artist's work was omitted simply because the submitted images were not clear enough, with proper lighting and exposure, for inclusion in the gallery. And yes, one determining factor in the final selection was quality of the photograph submitted. Difficult decisions were made by Terry Taylor and myself while hunched over a light box, loupes in hand, attempting to narrow a wide selection of submitted images down to those included in this book.

And don't be discouraged by what may feel like a personal rejection from a publisher; your work might not fill the need for one particular style of book, but may well be a lovely fit for another. Remain original! Follow your own true path. Imitate not. How lovely a feeling it is, when sharing one's artwork with another, to honestly say that the design is truly of one's own execution!

I'm honored to be associated with the many fine artists whose work graces the pages of this volume, and look forward to meeting each and every one of you in person, out there in the world beyond a snow-covered view that has altered my life on this one winter's day.

Nina Bagley

The Basics

HISTORY

Altered art is not a new art form. Artists have been altering art (unintentionally or otherwise) for a long time. In the monasteries of the Middle Ages, monks would sometimes copy new text over older parchment manuscripts. Parchment was too precious to throw away, so it was recycled. When the earlier writing on the manuscripts was incompletely erased or covered over and still visible these works became known as *palimpsests*.

In later centuries it was common practice for artists to paint over earlier, less important paintings or portions of paintings. Rubens, Titian, and even Leonardo da Vinci painted over earlier images they'd created. Later on, canvases by unknown or unrecognized artists were painted over by professional artists, amateurs, and forgers. When the underlying image shows through it's called *pentimento*.

The Victorians' obsession with memorializing the dead and their love of material objects found natural expression in the scrapbooks they created. Layers of memorabilia, cutouts from news magazines, calling cards, and greeting cards were lovingly pasted into albums collectors seek out today.

In the early years of the twentieth century, Pablo Picasso (1881–1973) and Georges Braque (1882–1963) expanded the language of a painting by incorporating fragments of newspaper, tickets, and other found objects into their work. After the first world war, artists associated with the Dada movement, such as Kurt Schwitters (1887–1948), worked exclusively with bits of discarded papers, random words, and chance imagery. Marcel Duchamp (1887–1968) exhibited both found objects (a bottle rack) and minimally altered objects (a bicycle wheel mounted on a stool). Many of these works, ridiculed or misunderstood at the time, have now become icons of modern art.

Late Victorian scrapbook

In midcentury, Joseph Cornell (1903–1972) created exquisite box constructions using pasted papers from bygone eras, photographic reproductions, natural materials, and found objects. In his basement home studio on Utopia Parkway in Queens, New York, he quietly built boxes with a craftsman's attention to construction and assembled them with a poet's eye for fine detail and juxtaposition. They are, without question, masterworks.

In the 1960s the work of Robert Rauschenberg (1925-), Jasper Johns (1930-), James Rosenquist (1933-), and Andy Warhol (1928–1987) used the images of pop culture—soup cans, magazine illustrations, flags, and comic books—in both painting and sculpture. Working in the same time period, Joe Brainard (1942–1994) admired all of the "old masters," from Leonardo da Vinci to Goya and Manet, as well as the new old masters, from Picasso to de Kooning and Warhol. In his collage for *ArtNews*, he appropriated the image of Ernie Bushmiller's (1905–1982) comic strip character Nancy. She is presented as the beaming *Mona Lisa*, with her multiple heads topping Duchamp's *Nude Descending a Staircase*, and calling for help as she drowns in a sea of Jackson Pollock. This little-known work is both thought-provoking and hilarious at the same time.

JOSEPH CORNELL, American, 1903-1972, Untitled (called *"Hôtel de la Duchesse-Anne"*), stained, glazed, wooden box with paper backing for a kinetic assemblage of wood, paint, wood and paper bird, clippings, postage stamps, clock spring, metal rod, toy bracelet, rubber ball and painted bingo chips, 1957, 44.8 x 31.1 x 11.1 cm, The Lindy and Edwin Bergman Joseph Cornell Collection,1982. 1868 front view
Photograph © 1999, The Art Institute of Chicago, All Rights Reserved.

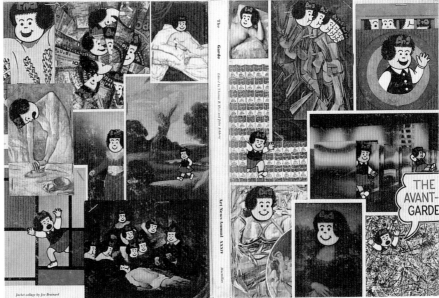

JOE BRAINARD, *Back and Front covers of Artnews Annual 34*, 1968, 12 x 9 in. (30.5 x 22.9 cm), Courtesy of the Estate of Joe Brainard and the Tibor de Nagy Gallery.

Allée des Cocotiers à Bonna

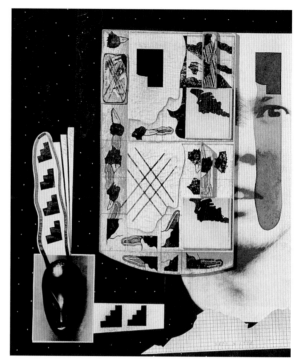

Before his death at age 31, Donald Evans (1945–1977) created a body of work with faux postage stamps he meticulously painted in watercolors. These stamps from wholly imaginary countries are perforated and individually canceled with hand-carved rubber stamps. He painted entire panes of stamps, as well as single stamps, that he affixed to vintage postcards.

Ray Johnson (1927–1995) explored the blurred lines between the twentieth century's popular and elite cultural icons in collages, books, and his prolific mail art correspondence. Greatly influenced by Duchamp and others, he was fond of wordplay and witty visual juxtapositions. He often added his own visage and quirky drawings to collages and postcard mailings.

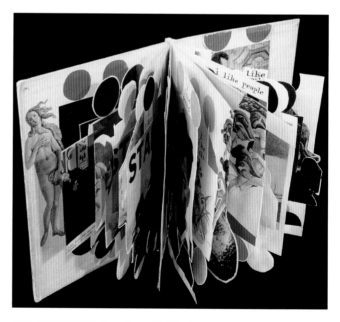

Recognized as one of the leading fiber artists of the twentieth century, Lenore Tawney (1907-) is well known for her innovative weaving and fiber installations. In the 1960s, paper and text became a focus of much of her work. Exquisite collages, assemblages, mail art, and artist books incorporate both found and specially created text. Her innovative works have influenced many artists.

LENORE TAWNEY, *Dear Lenore*, 1985-1990. 5½ x 4 x 3⅜ in. (14 x 10.2 x 8.6 cm). Book, letters, photographs, ribbon, bone fragment. Photo by George Erml.

In the last two decades of the twentieth century both popular recording artists and serious composers have combined altered sounds and previously recorded music when creating their own work. Contemporary musicians mix random sounds and scraps of melody or rhythm from other sources to create new work. The composer and visual artist Christian Marclay (1955 -) has created altered, unplayable musical instruments, video performances, and collages of sewn-together album covers. His works mirror his use of sound in his musical compositions. In this digital age, his chosen materials for these collages are both modern and archaic at the same time.

Using found objects in combination with collage, assemblage, and other art or craft techniques is now an accepted method of working for many artists. Newer methods such as scanning, layering, and dithering are entering the vocabulary of working artists everywhere. It's impossible to escape the influence, if not the imagery itself, of artists who have created before us. Let's embrace it by acknowledging our debt and admiration to those who have had the same urge to create.

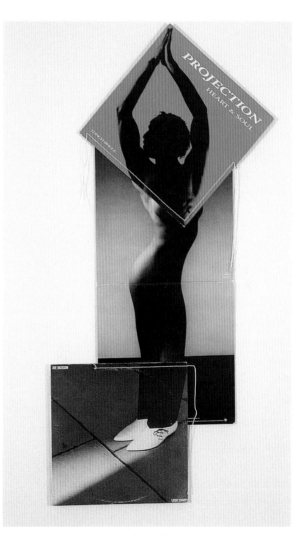

CHRISTIAN MARCLAY, *Look Sharp! (from the series 'Body Mix')*, 1991, record covers and cotton thread, 40½ x 17 in. (101.25 x 42.5 cm).
Courtesy of the Paula Cooper Gallery, New York

IMAGERY, TEXT, AND OBJECT

Though you might assume otherwise, creating a piece of altered art isn't difficult nor is it particularly mysterious. It's really not so very different from any other creative project you might embark on such as a scrapbook page, quilt, or decorative painting. You follow the same creative path that winds along from inspiration to planning to the fun part—work.

Altered art is created using three primary elements: imagery, text, and object. Using techniques and materials from both the art and crafting worlds, we combine two or three elements in our efforts to create thought-provoking works that celebrate creativity and the human imagination.

Imagery

For the first time ever, images of art have become ephemeral, ubiquitous, insubstantial, available, valueless, free. They surround us in the same way as language surrounds us.

John Berger (1972), *Ways of Seeing*

Imagery—added to the surface you're altering—is an essential aspect of altered art. Images communicate to the viewer what we're trying to express in the pieces we create. Whether the images are created by you (original) or come from other sources (appropriated), they must work toward some purpose or meaning.

Creating or choosing imagery is an important step in the creative process. Relax. You don't have to be Michelangelo in order to create an original image. Each and every one of us is capable of drawing, even if we're uncomfortable with the end results. It doesn't matter if we think the drawing is awful (we've all felt that way), even an awkward stick figure scrawled on a page will speak to the viewer. (Is it smiling, crouching, or crying?) The marks we make to draw that figure create meaning.

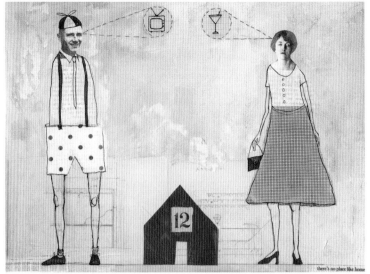

CLAUDINE HELLMUTH, *There's No Place Like Home*, 2003
Collage, acrylic paint, ink drawing; sewn, 18 x 24 in. (45.7 x 61 cm)

This is part of a new series of work in which I am trying to bring more of my hand to the work, by drawing the quirky figures instead of using only pre-printed materials.

And don't discount those stacks of out-of-focus or off-kilter snapshots that you've hidden away, either. Your photographs don't have to look like the photography of Ansel Adams to be usable. You'll be surprised at the imagery you can glean even from out-of-focus family vacation photos. Remember that trip you took to the desert last year? How about those snapshots your parents or grandparents made on their honeymoon in 1948?

Sources of Imagery

If you choose not to create original images (i.e., you feel you can't or just plain won't) you're probably wondering how you will come up with imagery. Lucky for you, we live in a world awash in visual imagery. It's all around us.

Having a wide selection of imagery on hand to choose from and use is a wonderful treasure. I have a fat three-ring binder, filled to overflowing with things I use in my own work: everything from anatomy illustrations (hands and heads, especially) to images of saints and the instructional photos from old Red Cross water safety and first aid manuals (to say nothing of the ten boxes that are filled with vintage and not-so-vintage postcard imagery). As you work, you'll find different types and styles of imagery that appeal to you. Start saving them now.

Sources of vintage imagery

I save imagery from old, out-of-print books, magazines, and art catalogs I've purchased in secondhand shops and antique stores. For years I kept a 12-volume set of *Lives of the Saints* and learned the hard way that attempting to save whole books (or sets of books) for imagery takes up valuable shelf space. I don't feel guilty stripping books of their images and neither should you if you choose to do so. And I'm not averse to using the original imagery in a piece I'm working on, rather than using a photocopy. Sometimes, it's just the right thing to do.

Clip-art imagery offers a wealth of possibilities. There are online sources for clip art and published books filled with copyright-free imagery. Rubber stamp imagery is simply astounding in its variety. And if you aren't up to the task of shopping for vintage imagery, many companies are marketing facsimiles of vintage imagery to choose from.

Your sources for imagery are boundless. Here's the real question: Is it okay to use the imagery you clipped from a magazine or found online or in an out-of-print book? Like all of life's crucial questions, the answer is both no and yes.

As you know, copyright is the legal right granted to an artist for exclusive use (including sale, publication, or distribution) of his creative work. In other words, as the creator I can do whatever I want with the work I've created (see page 20). Frankly, none of us would be happy if others took credit for or profited from our creative work. Especially without our knowledge or permission.

Speaking as an artist who uses appropriated imagery, here's my personal opinion: Visual artists far more gifted than I have created works that speak eloquently to me. I don't claim their works as my own. I may use an historic image as a starting point for a piece, or use a portion of an image in the same way an author might use a quote from another author to illustrate an idea or strengthen an argument. Joe Brainard's image on page 11 illustrates my point quite well.

What's most important, I think, is choosing the imagery. First, and foremost, the imagery must speak to you. If it doesn't speak to you, it won't elicit the response you intend from your viewer. For instance, don't use just any image of a house. Be deliberate and single-minded in your pursuit of the perfect image. A brick, split-level sitting in a manicured expanse of lawn and an ivy-covered Victorian gingerbread cottage elicit very different responses.

Modern reprints of vintage imagery

Image Transfer Methods

Adding images to a surface is probably the most intriguing part of creating altered art. It's also a daunting prospect for many people. There's a wide array of processes to choose from for use on almost any surface you can think of. Chances are you already have a preferred method you've used in previous crafting projects.

There are two basic questions you need to ask yourself once you've selected an image to transfer.

• What surface am I working on? Is it wood, paper, metal, plastic, or fiber?

• How do I want the finished image to look? Do I want an opaque image that sits on the surface or a transparent image that allows the original surface or background elements to appear through it?

Once you answer both questions, you're ready to choose a process.

Using Collage

Collage—simply cutting out an image and adhering it to a surface—works well for most materials. Use the original images or color photocopies. Collaged images are opaque. If you want a transparent or translucent image, you'll need to use a different type of transfer technique. Paper, wood, fiber, and even glass are suitable surfaces for collage.

 Designer Tip

If you have a black-and-white vintage image but don't have access to a color copier, you can approximate the aged appearance of the original. Make a black and white photocopy and stain it with strong tea, coffee, or walnut-base inks.

Using Rubber Stamps

With the appropriate ink, you can use rubber stamps on any surface. Stamps are child's play to use, but, oh, the sophisticated effects you can achieve with them. Layer images atop one another, mask portions of the image, or use embossing pigments for dimensional effects. Pigment inks, dye-base inks, and solvent-base inks are available in a wide palette of colors. Each ink type has its specific use recommended by the manufacturer printed on the packaging.

TERRY TAYLOR, *With Apologies to F-111* (left); *Listen Up!* (right), 2003
Magazine imagery on bridal shower bingo cards, 5 1/2 x 6 3/4 in. (14 x 17 cm)
Photo by Steve Mann

Hand-carved rubber stamp image by Susan McBride

If you can't find the rubber stamp you envision using, choose an image that will suit your needs and take it to a rubber stamp manufacturer (usually your local sign shop). For a nominal cost, they will make a custom-sized stamp for you.

For an original hand-crafted appearance, create your own one-of-a-kind rubber stamp. You'll find all of the materials you'll need—soft, vinyl printing blocks and linoleum gouges—in a craft or art supply store. Simply sketch or transfer an image to the block and carve away portions of the block that you don't wish to print (page 50).

Using Solvents

Black-and-white photocopies and clay-based (slick) magazine pages transfer to absorbent surfaces (paper, wood, and fabric) using the solvent transfer technique. The solvent breaks down the toners and inks on the paper and transfers the image to the surface. This transfer technique is not foolproof; results vary depending on the image and solvents used. The transferred image is transparent and has a soft, painterly appearance.

There are a number of different solvents to use. Some solvents—acetone, toulene-based markers, and lighter fluid—require adequate ventilation when you use them. Nontoxic solvents include oil of wintergreen and citrus-based solvents.

The transfer process is straightforward. Lay your image face down and lightly coat the reverse of the image with the solvent of your choice. Burnish or rub the paper with a bone folder, spoon, or similar tool. As you work, periodically lift a corner of the image to check transfer progress.

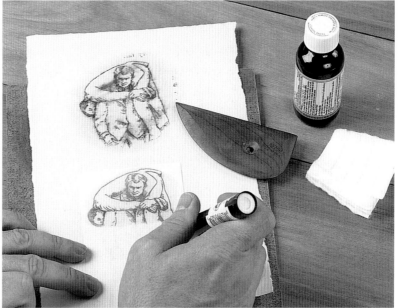

Using Heat Transfers

These transfer papers allow you to transfer an image you've printed on them onto a surface using heat. Most copy shops will make heat transfers for you. You can also find heat transfer papers for your home or office ink-jet printer. Heat transfers are applied face down and ironed onto your surface. Keep in mind that you'll need to create a mirror image copy if your image has text or if you want your image oriented in a certain direction. Heat transfers are best suited for fabric but can be used on paper. The image is opaque and sits on the surface.

TERRY TAYLOR
Ritual Pennant, 2000
Pennant, heat transfer image, antique bullion fringe, mica, thread,
13 x 21 in. (33 x 53.4 cm)
Collection of Marthe LeVan
Photo by Robert Chiarito

Using Water Slide Decals

Water slide decals are versatile, transparent image transfers that you can use on almost any type surface. Purchase commerically printed decals or create your own using water slide transfer paper. You can purchase the transfer paper for use with ink-jet printers or most types of toner-based photocopiers. Carefully follow the manufacturer's instructions for best results.

• Copy an image onto the transfer paper. Cut out the image and soak it in water.

• Carefully, slide the image off the backing paper onto the surface.

• Lightly burnish the image with a squeegee or foam brush to smooth the decal and remove any air trapped under the decal.

You'll need to prepare paper surfaces with one or two coats of acrylic medium before you apply this type of transfer. Transferring images to wood surfaces usually requires the use of a solvent such as turpentine. You can apply the transfer directly onto glass, metal, plastic, or ceramic surfaces. The image is baked onto heatproof surfaces for permanent application. Specially formulated transfer material is made for fabrics.

Using Acrylic Medium Transfers

Apply acrylic mediums to photocopied images using the technique that follows. These transfers are translucent and sit on top of the surface they're applied to.

• Lay a black-and-white or color photocopy face up on a piece of glass. Tape the image to the glass. Brush the image with successive coats of acrylic medium, letting each coat dry before applying the next. Anywhere from 5 to 12 coats may be applied. The more coats you apply, the thicker your transfer will be.

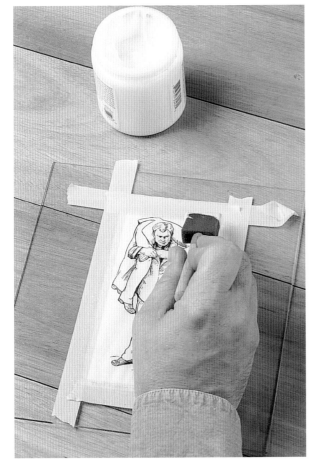

• After the layers of medium are thoroughly dry, remove the taped image from the glass. Soak the coated image in water and peel off the paper backing.

• Use your fingers or a sponge to roll the remaining layers of paper from the transfer. Don't rub too vigorously—the moist transfer will easily stretch or tear.

• Allow the transfer to dry, then apply the transfer to any surface with acrylic medium.

Making Packing Tape Transfers

Tape transfers are a quick, low-tech, and solvent-free way to place an image on a page. The end result is translucent and looks like a sticker.

• Place a glossy magazine picture or photocopy face down onto the sticky side of a strip of clear packing tape.

• Place the image face down on a hard surface. Burnish the back of the image vigorously with a bone folder or spoon.

• Remove the paper backing by dabbing the paper with a damp sponge. Allow the paper to absorb the water, then rub off the paper backing with your fingers.

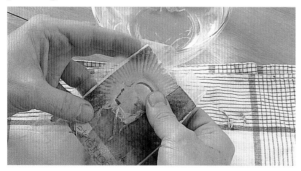

• If you'd prefer a matte finish—instead of a glossy finish—lightly sand the surface of the tape with a fine-grade sandpaper. Apply the transfer to your surface with an acrylic medium.

Copyright Issues

Many collage artists believe their work is exempt from copyright law. Several myths surround the legal status of collage and altered art. The most common myth is that collage is considered "fair use" under the law—that copyright restrictions don't apply when collage artists use images and text that they haven't created in a piece. Fair use protects only educational, critical, journalistic, research, and scholarly uses of copyrighted work.

The law considers all four of the following when determining whether it's fair (and legal) to use copyrighted materials:

• *Is it used for commercial or for nonprofit educational purposes?*

• *What is the nature of the copyrighted work?*

• *What is the amount and significance of the portion of the copyrighted work being used?*

• *What is the impact of the use on the potential market for the copyrighted work?*

Another myth is that it's okay to use only a small portion of copyrighted material, such as five or 10 percent. In reality, there is no magic number or percentage that can be taken from a copyrighted work in fair use. If you use only five percent of a photograph in your collage, but it is the five percent that lies at the heart of the original work—its very essence—you could find yourself ensnared in a legal morass.

A specific image that gives a photo its emotional impact cannot be used without permission. If you lock the collage in a closet, it still violates the law, even though police aren't likely to confiscate it. However, that also means that giving the collage or copies of it to your friends is illegal and publishing it may be asking for trouble. Remember, the law defines publication as distribution, which means handing out the collage for free, putting it in a book or magazine, or selling it.

A third myth is that any material published without a copyright notice or posted on the Internet is fair game. The law treats the Internet no differently from print publications, and the law since 1978 says that any work is automatically copyrighted once it is created in tangible form. Planning a work of art in your head is not enough, but once it is painted, photographed, or typed into a computer, it is copyrighted. Collage has no special protection under the law, although many artists believe otherwise. The only safe way to use copyrighted materials in your collage or altered art are to get written permission from the copyright holder, or to use your own original materials instead.

Text

Artists have been adding text to their works since the invention of written language. Text may be added to identify an image or to convey additional meaning. It can be easily read or obscured. Like imagery, it should be chosen with intent.

There are many ways to generate text, if you wish to use it in your altered art. Create word lists, check collections of quotes, use personal journal entries, or clip phrases that appeal to you from the magazines and newspapers you read. I purchase old dictionaries for both imagery and text.

Using an Internet search engine is a wonderful way to find text. I found links to long-forgotten poems I had read (and loved) in school and a fragment of a song lyric I hadn't thought of in years when I was working on the altered book cover on page 60.

How to Add Text

The easiest way to add text to a piece is to simply write it yourself. This conveys a sense of immediacy and adds a human touch. However, many people feel about their handwriting the same way they feel about their ability to draw. Here are some options you can use if you wish to add text to a piece you're working on.

ROXENE ROCKWELL, *I Am the Man in the Box*, 1997
Wood box; assemblage, collage, 12½ x 7½ x 4 in.
(31.8 x 19 x 10.2 cm)
Photo by Bruce Brown

This is a Ken doll covered with the "date ads" that describe who the man looking for a date is. "I do dishes" is collaged on his left hand and "romance minded" is on his forehead.

Dictionaries are sources for both text and imagery

You can use transfer techniques for text as well. The only thing to remember is that if you are using a transfer technique that is placed face down (heat transfers, solvent transfers, and some water slide transfers) your text will be reversed. Reversed text can be intriguing visually, but it might not be the effect you're after. If it isn't, use the mirror options on your photocopier when you create your text.

Objects

What can you alter? The answer is simple: anything and everything. You may prefer to work solely on book pages or in boxes. How do you select an object? At the risk of sounding mystical, objects speak to the artist in some manner: either through their shape, texture, material, or by association.

Objects have meaning. Meaning may be defined by use, material, or association. A spoon is more than just a spoon. Spoons stir the batter. Spoons feed. Silver spoons speak of wealth. Perforated spoons can't hold water. By altering objects, we can create new meaning and associations for them.

As human beings we all have (to one degree or another) a bit of the magpie in us. We surround ourselves with objects whether we admit it or not.

There are many styles and sizes of rubber stamp alphabets in the world. In addition, you can choose from stamps with foreign phrases and words or phrases written in foreign script.

Use clippings from printed texts, transfer lettering, stickers, metal letters, and game pieces to add text to your pieces. If you have access to an old-fashioned typewriter, type your text. Typewritten text on paper feels entirely different than computer-generated text, even with the wide selection of computer fonts you can use.

An eclectic selection of lettering choices

Look around your own living or work space. You'll see things (no matter how large or small) that you've surrounded yourself with. And why? Because they speak to you.

Speaking for myself, I think it's true that people who are creating altered art or want to create altered art are inexplicably drawn to objects. We purchase them on impulse or avidly seek them out. We may know exactly what to do with an object we've purchased. Or, it may sit on the shelf for longer than we care to admit, until one day inspiration hits us.

Objects can be altered and objects can be used as materials for altering, as well. Again, anything and everything is fair game. Whether you purchase the objects in a craft or antiques store, find them on the street, or have them stashed away, you'll amass small objects of all shapes, sizes, and materials as you work.

If you're drawn to altered art, you're no doubt already on the way to having materials to work with. It goes with the territory. You know what materials and embellishments you've stored. Don't discount any of them. They can all be used. Maybe not right away, but one day (believe me) you'll want one specific thing and you'll be glad you saved it.

One of the aspects of creating altered art that I'm particularly drawn to is the collaborative aspect. I try to be as free in sharing my unique collections of objects as I hope others will be with me in return.

Scrapbooking embellishments, found objects, and natural materials

Stumped?

Creativity is the power to connect the seemingly unconnected.
WILLIAM PLOMER

It happens to all of us as we create things. There are times when you see in your mind's eye the form, imagery, and materials you need to create a piece of altered art. At other times you're stumped, have no idea where you're headed, or how to get there.

Inspiration, no matter how mystical and effortless it may appear to be when it happens to someone else, is more often the result of work. There is no single, correct step-by-step method for getting inspired. You'll create your own methods for gaining insight and inspiration as you work. Try using any of these working tips when you're stumped

Take Time to Think

Thinking is working. Give yourself permission and time to do it. Put on your favorite music, take a leisurely stroll, or quietly wash the dishes by hand. Set aside even small periods of time to ruminate about the piece you're working on or projects you have in mind for the future. If something comes to mind that interests you, jot it down or roughly sketch it in a notebook right away. Otherwise, chances are good that you won't remember that flash of insight or inspiration when you need it later on.

Give yourself a break from thinking about pieces you're working on if nothing satisfying or intriguing comes to mind. You know the old saying about beating a dead horse.

Think about something else or work on something completely different. Inspiration will come at odd moments—as you're picking up the dry cleaning or just before falling asleep. I like to keep my notebook close at hand, just in case.

Create Text

What words or phrases do you associate with your piece? Grab a pencil and paper, or fire up that laptop. Write words randomly as they come to you. Don't stop to question your choice of specific words. Creating a random list of words can take you on strange but useful journeys you might not have taken otherwise.

Computers are useful tools for taking us on those strange journeys. Type a phrase into an Internet search engine and you'll be amazed at what you find. Links to a poem, song lyrics, or book titles may jog your memory or take you to places (and information) that might not have occurred to you when you began your search.

Choose Imagery

Go to the library and check out art books to read or look at. Even better, give yourself time to gather a stack, find yourself a comfortable place to sit, and look at the books without distraction. Choose a book about an artist you admire or discover the work of someone unknown to you. Read the sidebar on pages 32 and 33 for my personal recommendations.

Log on to the Internet and look for clip art images that interest you. Spend some time in a local museum or visit the great museums of the world online: The Metropolitan, The Louvre, or The Prado. It's cheaper than buying an airline ticket (but not nearly as satisfying, alas).

Leaf through magazines you own and cut out images that appeal to you. File them in folders for future use.

If you generated a list of words for text, you probably unconsciously visualized images at the same time (the human brain works that way). Look for images that illustrate the words.

Meditative Rummaging

Admit it: You have stuff. Hidden in boxes, piled on shelves, or tucked neatly into files. I'm of two minds about my own stuff—there's either too much or there's never enough. Take your pick. Get out those boxes of trinkets, decorative papers, or image files and rummage through them. (It's one of my favorite things to do.) You'll find things you've forgotten about and can look at them in a new light. If questioned about what you're doing, you can always say you're tidying up.

Pull out the things you're thinking of using for a piece and set them aside. I have small piles on my worktable for pieces I'm working on or pondering for the future.

If you don't have the right stuff (the materials you envision using for your project), go to the craft store, flea market, or secondhand store; clean out your garage or ask a friend if you can rummage through her stuff. When I envisioned certain materials for projects for this book, I visited an online auction service and found precisely what I was looking for at a reasonable price.

Limit Your Choices

You may be overwhelmed by the vast selection of materials, colors, or objects available to use in your piece. If so, use only a color you like or, even more challenging, one you don't like! Select a single image and manipulate it in as many ways as you can think of rather than using several images. Choose only one or two embellishments—fiber, paper, or dimensional objects—before you begin work. It's easy to add elements, more difficult to select elements to remove.

Take Time for Work

Choose a set time for working on a piece. The early morning light in my work space makes the first part of the day one of my favorite times to work. Even meditative rummaging or thinking during the set-aside time counts as work.

Try working in small increments of time. Limit yourself to half an hour and create a simple background color on a piece. When time is up, walk away and do something else (there are always chores to do) or work on a different piece altogether. This gives you time to consider the piece you're working on and allow the piece to develop slowly without being forced.

Don't feel pressured to finish a piece in one work session. Arrange elements on a page but don't attach them. Let them sit overnight. You'll either like the results in the morning or rearrange those elements in a more satisfying way.

By all means, give in to the joy of working on a piece if inspiration strikes and you just can't stop! Be thankful for that time—it's a gift.

Creative Play

When I'm stuck and can't make progress on a piece, I indulge in a little creative play. I keep a stack of blank greeting cards and a selection of paper scraps near my work table. I pull out three or four scraps of paper and create an abstract collage on a single card or a series of cards. I'm not making art, I'm exercising my urge to create and having a little fun at the same time.

Other artists work in notebooks, art journals, or alter pages in books they've set aside just for creative play. Create trading cards, alter postcards, doodle aimlessly, or do whatever else you can think of. Rest assured, the answer to your creative dilemma will come to you when you least expect it.

Ricordo di Taranto

"When I take a week's vacation at the beach for Thanksgiving I always pack a small project to work on or a few materials to work with "just in case." In this case—armed with only a postcard booklet, an old dictionary, glue, and scissors—I created an altered book any surrealist would be proud of."

Terry Taylor, DESIGNER

1. I chose an illustrated dictionary for imagery. The pages had yellowed with age, which complemented the sepia tones of the postcard booklet.

2. I randomly thumbed through the dictionary, choosing images that I found interesting, such as an eel or a mop (illustrating the verb swab), a centaur, architectural elements, a Turkish flag, a dirigible, and a parachute. None of the images had anything at all to do with the images in the booklet.

3. I roughly trimmed the images before placing them on pages at random. Moving images from page to page is the fun part of the exercise. Does the centaur look better prancing on the plaza or crossing a bridge? When I was satisfied with the image placement, I trimmed each one and glued it to the page.

4. As I waited for the glued images to dry, I went for a walk on the beach.

A selection of useful tools

USEFUL TOOLS

Every artist and crafter has a collection of favorite, essential tools. You may have a pair of scissors you've set aside just for cutting paper. I'm very fond of a specific brand of number three pencil for sketching and writing. And if I can't find my small, brass pencil sharpener in the depths of my tote bag to sharpen my pencil with, I am not a happy camper.

The following list may seem obvious, but each item is an indispensable tool for creative work.

A blank **sketchbook** is handy. Use one as a personal art journal for rough sketches of project ideas. Glue in bits of paper or imagery for inspiration and try out new techniques or materials. Copy quotes that interest or inspire you (be sure you add their sources for future reference). Compile any lists you make while working (see page 24). But don't succumb to the day-to-day necessity of jotting down the grocery or errand list on these pages; use scrap paper for those! Doodle on the pages and use them to jog your memory when you're at a creative stand-still. You don't have to share this book with anyone. It's yours and yours alone!

Pencils (or pens if you prefer) are practical and versatile tools for sketching, writing, and mark-making of all sorts. Keep both graphite and colored pencils on hand, along with your favorite pens.

Use catalogs, old magazines (the kind that don't have interesting photos!), or last year's phone book as surfaces for gluing or painting. Open to a clean page, apply your adhesive or paint, and turn the page when you need a fresh page to work on. When you're finished, put the whole, glued-together mess in the recycling bin.

Self-healing **cutting mats** extend the life and protect the beauty of your worktable. My dining room table still bears more than a few scars from the days when I didn't have a cutting mat. If you're working on a book, you can slip a mat behind a page to protect the remaining pages. In a pinch, use cardboard or a magazine to protect your working surface when you cut.

Cutting tools—scissors of all types and a craft knife—are very essential tools. Keep a pair of everyday scissors on hand, as well as an assortment of decorative-edge scissors and a pair of small, sharp-pointed scissors reserved solely for precision cutting. Be sure to keep a supply of sharp blades on hand for your craft knife; you'll achieve precise and smooth cuts with a sharp blade. If you're working with specific materials such as metal or wood, you'll need cutting tools just for those materials. Whatever you do, don't use a cutting tool for a material it wasn't intended to cut. Even if the tool is handy and will cut the material, use the correct tool for the job.

Keep **brushes** of all sizes and types near your worktable. There's nothing more pleasing to look at than a container chock-full of a variety of brushes. Use them for painting and stippling, varnishing or gluing. Like any other tool, keep your brushes in good working condition by cleaning them thoroughly after you use them. Acrylic mediums and paints dry more quickly than you think. Keep a container of water nearby to soak your brushes until you can clean them.

A **bone folder** is the perfect tool for crisply creasing folds or burnishing. If you don't own one, use the back of a spoon or the dull side of a table knife. You also can use wooden or hard plastic pottery tools.

Keep **adhesives**—from an all-purpose white glue to two-step epoxies—on hand. If you're wondering what type of adhesive to use with a material you're thinking of working with, read the section on adhesives on pages 31 and 32.

Rulers that have a metal edge and cork-backed metal rulers of any size are useful in a great number of ways. It's nearly impossible to cut or draw a perfectly straight line without one.

Waxed paper is technically a material, but it's also a multipurpose tool. Use it to protect work surfaces when you're applying glue or paint. Sandwich painted or glued book pages between sheets before you press them flat. Use waxed paper as a see-through mask. Spray a thin coat of adhesive on the paper and apply it to the area to be masked.

JEN SWEARINGTON
Art Journals, 1999 – 2003.
Photo by Steve Mann

Art journals don't have to start out as blank books. Jen works directly on the printed pages of well-worn books.

MISCELLANEOUS MATERIALS AND TOOLS

Coloring Materials

What are your favorite coloring materials? Fluid inks, acrylic paints, markers, pencils, pastels, gouaches, encaustics, or stamping inks? Your favorites are reliable, predictable, and comfortable to use. But don't get stuck in a rut and use the same kind for every project. Branch out.

New and exciting coloring materials appear on the market with regularity. Use your notebook or create an art journal specifically for color experiments. If you like the new materials, you'll add them to your bag of coloring tricks and continue to use them. It's never a good idea to try new coloring materials (or techniques) on a project before you've tested them.

Use any coloring materials to create your altered art. As long as the material is compatible with your surface, you can use it. Some surfaces— plastic, glass, or metal—may need special consideration. Follow your instincts, and when in doubt, read the label on a new coloring material. Oil-based paints can be used but not in altered books as a rule. Oil paints—and by extension oil pastels—take too long to completely dry.

Unique paper items, tags, and modern copies of vintage material

Papers

It's wonderful to have a large selection of papers on hand, but it can also be overwhelming. I try (note: try is the operative word here) to keep mine sorted by type: handmade papers in one file, patterned papers in another. Buying papers—like buying fabric or yarn—is a harmless addiction. Nevertheless, it's an addiction many of us struggle with.

I always find the wide variety of Asian papers alluring when I visit a specialty paper store. Corrugated paper, handmade papers with inclusions, translucent vellums, patterned papers for scrapbooking, and novelty papers that are flocked or gilded: I want them all, even if I don't have an immediate use for them.

And don't forget to add bits of recycled papers to your stash. Save those charming tea labels, foil wrappers, and chopstick envelopes. They'll come in handy if you're judicious in saving them. Try to save only those that are really unique and special. Otherwise, your work space will be overrun.

Other Tools

Keep a variety of tape on hand. In addition to cellophane tape, be sure you have masking and clear packing tape. Masking tape is useful for protecting areas from paint (see page 131), and packing tape can be used to create image transfers (see page 20). Double-sided tapes are useful as well.

Staples, brads, small wire brads, nails, and even thumbtacks can be used to attach things to a variety of surfaces. Eyelets and grommets are multipurpose fasteners for fabric, paper, and craft metals. Pop rivets and a pop rivet tool are useful when you're working with heavier pieces of metal (see page 127).

Tools you own for household maintenance such as a hammer, small saw, pliers, wire cutters, a drill, and drill bits may be useful for some projects. Use a heat gun (for removing paint) to speed the drying process of painted surfaces or activate embossing powders. A hair dryer will work just as well if you don't have one.

Keep hole punches of all shapes and sizes, or at least an awl on hand for making holes in various materials from paper to wood and metal. Straight pins and needles make tiny holes. If you don't have any on hand, buy a travel sewing kit. Should you decide to stitch something on your altered art you'll need it.

GLUES AND ADHESIVES

Along with the favorite tools and materials you use, you'll likely have a glue or adhesive that you turn to time and time again. When you're working with a surface you've not used before, you may need to use a glue you've not used before. It's always a good idea to check the label for recommended applications—especially when using a glue you're not familiar with.

While you're reading the label, keep two questions in mind. Are my surfaces porous or non-porous? Do I want a strong, long-lasting bond or a temporary bond? Once you've answered these questions, you can determine whether the glue you're considering is right for the job.

White Glues
White glues are widely used for all types of craft applications. They're readily found in most households. These all-purpose glues are (usually) water soluble, clear drying, and somewhat flexible. You can use them on almost all surfaces from paper to ceramics and fabric to some plastics. They're not recommended for use on metals or anything that will come in contact with water.

Many—if not most—white glues are PVA glues (polyvinyl acetate adhesive).

You can find many different brands with consistencies that range from thin to thick. In general, these glues can be thinned with water as desired.

Acrylic Mediums
Acrylic mediums are made of polymer emulsions. When dry, they form durable, flexible, nonyellowing films. They're the binder (glue) of acrylic paint that holds the paint pigment. Mediums are available in different viscosities and sheens. In general, you can use acrylic mediums with paper and other porous surfaces as you would most white glues.

Hot Glue
Hot glue bonds quickly and works well on both porous and nonporous surfaces. It works especially well for bonding uneven surfaces to each other. Don't use this glue for structural purposes (the bond is easily broken) and limit its use with paper projects.

Cyanoacrylate Glues
These are the wonder glues of the modern world. Adjectives like *super* or *crazy* usually mean the glue is a cyanoacrylate glue. Just a drop (literally!) usually does the trick. They are fast-bonding, clear, and strong. Surfaces must fit tightly in order for these glues to work well. Their power is wasted on paper crafts, and they may not work well with some plastics.

Industrial Strength Adhesives
Two-part epoxies, jewelry glues, silicone glues, china glues, multipurpose cements, and contact adhesives all fall into this category. They all offer a strong bond for hard-to-glue materials such as metals, ceramics, rubber, fiberglass, plastics, and glass. They

dry clear and can sometimes be used as sealants as well. When working with them provide plenty of ventilation and carefully follow the manufacturer's instructions.

Spray Adhesives

These adhesives are great for covering large, flat surfaces such as papers and fabrics. Use them in well-ventilated areas with your work area covered to protect from overspray. They are repositionable. If you want a more permanent bond you can coat both surfaces to be joined and allow them to become tacky or dry before joining. Just follow the manufacturer's recommendations.

Wood Glues

Wood glues are generally divided into two types: AR (aliphatic resin) and polyurethane glues. AR adhesives are common yellow wood glues that are for interior use. Polyurethane glues are fine for both interior and exterior uses.

Glue Sticks

These glues are usually acid-free and specifically formulated for use on paper, cardboard, fabric, and photographs. Some are permanent; others are repositionable. In general, they dry clear and are less susceptible to wrinkling than more fluid glues.

DAYLE DOROSHOW
Thread of Shining Days, 2002
Glass jar, polymer clay,
paper, photocopy transfer; carved,
sculpted, 10 x 5 in. (25.4 x 12.7 cm)
Photo by Don Felton

Here are just a few of the books I can recommend to satisfy a craving for inspiration.

The Art of Assemblage
William C. Seitz
The Museum of Modern Art, New York
Doubleday and Company, Inc., 1961
An excellent historical reference from the early 1960s containing a wealth of black and white images of early works by well-known artists like Robert Rauschenberg and Louise Nevelson, and lesser-known (but nonetheless influential) artists such as Arman, George Herms, and Jess.

Collage, Assemblage, and the Found Object
Diane Waldman
Harry N. Abrams, Inc., 1992
The definitive history of collage and the found object. Richly illustrated with many little-known works.

An Illustrated Encyclopedia of Traditional Symbols
J.C. Cooper
Thames and Hudson, 1992
In Roman symbolism the pumpkin represented stupidity and madness. Red carnations, passionate love; yellow ones, rejection. This book is filled with interesting tidbits of information that will inspire you with both image and text.

The World of Donald Evans
Willy Eisenhart
Dial/Delacorte, 1980
Whimsical. Delicate. Enchanting. Step into Evans's finely drawn, imaginary philatelic world.

A Sampling of Inspirational Books

Symbols, Signs, and Signets
Ernst Lehner
Dover Publications, Inc., 1950
A treasure trove of visual stimulation. Graphic images from the realms of alchemy, heraldry, magic amulets, Japanese crests, and more.

Color: A Natural History of the Palette
Victoria Finlay
Ballantine Publishing Group, 2002
Did you know that yellow pigment was once made in India by feeding cattle a strict diet of mango leaves? How did the precious color blue travel from mines in Afghanistan to Michelangelo's brush? This books tells the fascinating history of color's physical materials.

Griffin & Sabine: An Extraordinary Correspondence
Nick Bantcock
Chronicle Books, 1991
Want to be ravished by drawings and collage? Enjoy a good story? This one is an old favorite, but you can pick any of this prodigious artist's works and be enthralled.

The Postcard Century: 2000 Cards and Their Messages
Tom Phillips
Thames & Hudson, 2000
A huge book (selected by the artist who created A Humument) documenting a century's worth of images. A must see.

Dime-Store Alchemy: The Art of Joseph Cornell
Charles Simic
The Ecco Press, 1992
Simic's short reflections on the works and life of Joseph Cornell are illuminating and inspiring. Perfect for bedtime reading.

Lenore Tawney Signs on the Wind
Holland Carter
Pomegranate, 2002
If you don't know Tawney's works, you'll be awed and inspired by their subtle beauty. You'll wish you were on her mailing list.

The Journey is the Destination
Dan Eldon
Chronicle Books, 1997
The visual diaries of a young news correspondent's last years in war-torn Somalia. Both moving and innovative.

Joseph Cornell: Shadowplay....Eterniday
Hartigan, Hopps, Vine, and Lehrman
Thames & Hudson, 2003
If you've ever dreamed of being able to play with one of Cornell's boxes, this is the book for you.

True Colors: A Palette of Collaborative Art Journals
Kathryn Bold
Independent Publishing Group, 2003
Fifteen artists. Fifteen art journals. Color is the theme for this visual feast of a round robin. You won't be disappointed.

Found Object Art
Dorothy Spencer
Schiffer Publishing, Ltd., 2002
An extensive gallery book featuring a wide selection of artists and craftsmen working exclusively with found objects.

Basics

Altering books has become a popular and widespread creative activity in the last several years, but it isn't a new one. A few fine artists have been altering books for decades. Their work is both innovative and inspirational.

Tom Phillips began *A Humument*—his influential work created on the pages of an obscure Victorian novel—in 1966. It was first brought into print in 1980 and has been reissued in revised editions as new work has been added to the text. Nick Bantcock's *Griffin & Sabine: An Extraordinary Correspondence* (1991) was a publishing phenomenon. The mysterious illustrated story captured the imagination of readers worldwide (see page 33).

In the last few years Internet groups and the websites of talented artists have contributed to the widespread popularity of the altered book as a medium for creative expression. Whether you're working on your own or with a group in a round robin exchange (see page 51), altering books can be a satisfying creative experience.

Altering books doesn't require a whole new set of skills. Many skills you use in art or craft projects will serve you well: rubber-stamping, collage, and simple painting techniques, to name just a few. You know how to do those things, but you'll need to add a few tricks to your repertoire when using books as a medium for your altered art.

TERRY TAYLOR
Kindergarten drawing, circa 1957
Crayon on paper, 8¼ x 14 in. (21 x 35.6 cm)
Photo by Steve Mann

Books to Use

A drawing I did in kindergarten of a fire-breathing dragon (or giraffe?) is pinned to the bulletin board in my office. (My mother saved everything; I am my mother's son.) It's a puzzling drawing. I have no memory of what prompted the text—*Do not cut your books!* It illustrates what we've all been taught: Books, as objects, are precious. And they are.

Books are vessels of knowledge, memory, and culture. I wouldn't dream of scrawling notes or cutting pages in a rare first edition of Whitman's *Leaves of Grass*. But I have no problem using a discarded book club edition or textbook as a base for creative exploration.

Secondhand stores, yard sales, and library book sales are prime sources of books, from novels to textbooks and comic books to composition books. If you're worried about damaging a true and rare first edition you might find, take it to a book dealer

for valuation. You can also do your own research on the Internet or consult books on collecting to help you out of this dilemma.

In my own experience with rare book dealers, I've learned that most old or well-known books don't have great value. Truth is, very few of them are valuable. Of course there's always someone somewhere who might want the book you've just purchased. Do you really want to worry about that? I wouldn't. Use your own good judgement and common sense.

Books are used either as substrates or springboards for altered art. When used as a substrate (simply put: the thing you alter), you impose your own theme and design on the printed pages. You may or may not choose to incorporate parts of the printed text and illustrations. When books are used as springboards, the illustrations, text, and perhaps the style of the book dictate what you will do to the book.

Save illustrations, but don't attempt to alter these books in this shape.

Choose a book that's sturdy and intact to work on. You can overlook dinged corners or some youthful scrawls made with a ballpoint pen. I wouldn't recommend trying to rebind a book whose spine is falling apart. And perhaps you really should pass on a book that smells of mildew, cigar smoke, or (heaven forbid!) an overly friendly feline. Hardbound books can take more handling and punishment than paperbacks. The sewn signatures (groups of pages)

DORIT ELISHA, *Tic-Tag-Toe: Documenting the Life of a Family Through Tags*, 2003
Card pocket wall panel, tags, tickets, 19 x 6 x 1 in. (48.3 x 15.2 x 2.5 cm)
Photo by Dotti Cichon

in hardbound books are more durable than the glued signatures of paperbacks.

Examine the pages of a book before you purchase it. Be on the lookout for pages printed on heavy stock; they're great to work on. The pages in older books are often too yellowed, fragile, and brittle to work on. That said, don't let an older book with illustrations you're particularly attracted to slip through your fingers. Buy the book and remove the illustrated pages. Toss the remnants in the trash or recycle them.

Children's board books are fine substrates for altering. Their thick board pages are a delight to work on. And consider altering other types of books: address books, checkbooks, receipt books, multi-sleeved record albums, ledgers, cookbooks, or folded postcard sets. A leather-bound passport might be the springboard for documenting an imaginary journey. In this case foreign stamps, currency, and portions of postcards would make fine page embellishments.

Create a record of imaginary travels.

Strengthening Pages

You can alter single pages in a book with simple collage, rubber-stamped images, or drawing with dry mediums such as a pencil or chalk. However, if you want to use fluid mediums, such as paints or inks, or wish to add heavy elements to your pages, you'll need to strengthen them to prevent wrinkling or tearing. Here are a few techniques you can use for strengthening pages. As you continue to work in altered books, you'll be able to pinpoint what technique to use with the mediums that you choose.

• Use a glue stick to hold two or three pages together. This is quick and easy. Run the glue stick right off the edges of the page. If you're worried about getting glue on other pages, slip a sheet of waxed paper behind the page you're gluing.

• Use your bone folder to smooth the glued pages together securely. Doing so helps eliminate any air pockets between the pages.

• Use an acrylic gel medium or white glue to build thicker page stacks. Medium is more fluid than a glue stick, so it's a good idea to protect the pages underneath with a sheet of waxed paper. Spread the medium on the page with a brush.

• To prevent the pages from wrinkling, use an old credit card or piece of cardboard to spread the medium in a very thin, even coat. Wipe the excess glue on the card onto a sheet of waxed paper. You can use the excess on the next page.

• Burnish the two glued pages together with your bone folder or smooth them with the clean edge of a credit card. Spread medium on top and add another page. Sandwich the glued pages between sheets of waxed paper, close the book, and press the pages until they are dry. Glue additional pages (three or four at a time) to the stack. If you allow your page-stack to dry in stages, it's less likely to wrinkle.

• Stitch a group of pages together with a simple blanket stitch, running stitch, or whipstitch. To make the sewing process easier, pierce the edges of the stacked pages with an awl or small hole punch. Thread your needle with silk thread, embroidery floss, narrow ribbon, or jute. Stitch the pages together, using the pierced holes as a guide. And don't limit yourself to traditional fibers: Sew with colored wire, plastic lacing, or shoelaces.

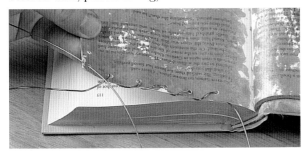

• For a different look, use brads, staples, or eyelets to hold a stack of pages together. You'll need to punch holes in the stack for brads or eyelets. If using eyelets, punch small holes the same size as your eyelets. Place an eyelet in a hole and turn the page over. I like to slip a thin piece of board under the page before I set the eyelet. Use a hammer and setting tool to spread the back of the eyelet. Repeat the process with each eyelet.

Creating Windows and Doors

You can add interest to your pages in a variety of ways. Create a tantalizing glimpse of the page that follows with a simple window, or hide an unexpected illustration behind a door that opens and closes.

Plan where a window or door needs to be placed on the page to showcase what's underneath effectively. Also consider the shape and size of your opening.

If you don't like what you've created simply use a sharp craft knife to remove the page and try it again.

KATIE METHENY, *Harriet Beecher Stowe*, 2003
Page spread with doors in *Liberated Women: Bluestockings and Socialist Women* by Daumier, 19 x 12½ in. (48.3 x 31.8 cm)
Photo by Steve Mann

An Easy Window

• You can create a very simple window in any shape using a decorative hole punch.

As you can see, the square hole punched out in the photo on the right didn't really work with the circular illustrations on the page. If I'd really been thinking ahead, I would have used a circular punch. I solved the problem by gluing a circular decorative trim over the square hole (see page 73).

A Simple Door

• Create a template shape for a door. To make your template absolutely symmetrical (as for the double door illustrated here), fold a sketched shape in half, then cut it out. Trace around the shape with a pencil directly onto the page.

• Be sure to protect the pages underneath your door before you cut it. Slip a cutting mat or a piece of cardboard under the page before you cut.

• Fold your a door's "hinge" against a metal edge ruler to ensure a sharp, straight fold.

• Position your chosen image on the following page after the door is cut to ensure accurate placement of the image.

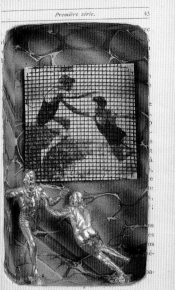

TERRY TAYLOR
Untitled, 1999
Gold leaf, action figures, screen wire, imagery,
5 x 7 x 1 in. (12.7 x 17.8 x 2.5 cm)
Collection of Chandler Gordon
Photo by Evan Bracken

Creating a Niche

Creating a niche for a dimensional object is not particularly difficult, but it does require both time and care to create a solid and well-crafted one. And it requires a little extra planning. What's going inside the niche? The depth of the niche will depend on what you want to place in it. What shape will you make your niche? Are you placing the niche in the beginning, center, or end of the book? Allow for plenty of drying time and be certain you have sharp craft knife blades handy. In the photos that follow, I'll show you how to create a niche placed at the end of a book.

• Estimate how deep you need your niche to be. Glue several of the last pages in the book onto the inside back cover. Then use several bulldog clips to hold together a block of pages slightly deeper than the niche you want to create.

• With the block of pages clipped together, paint the edges of the block with a coat of acrylic gel medium. You'll have to move the clips in order to coat all parts of the block's edge. Let the first coat dry. (You can hurry the drying process with a hair dryer). After the first coat has dried, the block should hold together. Remove the clips and coat the edges with additional applications of medium.

• Draw the shape of the niche on the top of the block.

• Cut out the marked shape using a sharp craft knife or box cutter. Hold the cutting tool against the metal edge of a ruler for best results. Cut through just a few pages at a time, remove the cut pages, and then cut through a few more. Repeat this process until the niche is as deep as you need it to be.

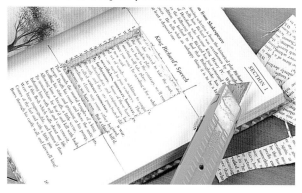

• Apply two or three coats of medium to the inside edges of the cut niche, then prepare your pages as needed. Here, I coated the pages with gesso to obscure the text, then added a layer of Oriental tissue to color the pages.

• I added origami paper inside the niche, rubber-stamped text, and placed a brass fish inside. I covered the niche with a photocopy transparency.

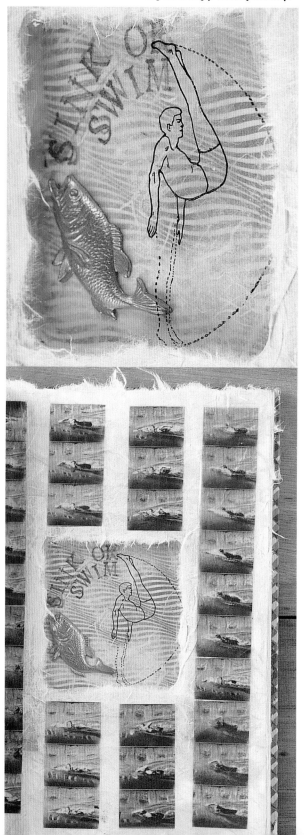

Folding and Cutting Pages

Pages in your books don't have to remain the shape you find them in. Fold or cut pages to add both visual and sculptural interest before you alter them further.

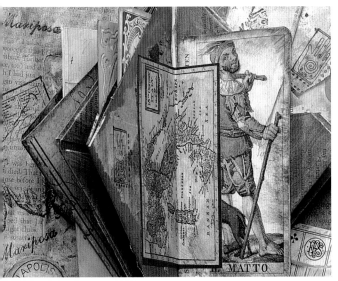

CAROL OWEN, Untitled, 2003
Altered book, paint, found objects, 7½ x 8¼ x ¾ in. (19 x 21 x 1.9 cm)
Photo by Seth Tice-Lewis

Folding

• Fold pages in half (thirds or quarters) or create pointed pages with diagonal folds. The folded pages will hide or reveal images as you choose. Glue the folds to strengthen the new page shapes.

• Add color and decorative papers to the pages. Adding decorative paper increases the thickness of these folded pages. If needed, remove a few adjacent pages with a sharp craft knife. Otherwise, the bulk of your folded and glued pages will prevent your book from closing as it did before.

• Here's a finished spread of folded pages. I used photocopies of vintage Japanese postcards, rubber-stamped text, and bits of other printed papers. The finished page spread mimics the intricate folds of a Japanese *obi* (kimono sash).

Cutting

• A book on the mysteries of the brain is the spring-board for these shaped pages. A template of a head in profile is traced onto the pages before they are cut. Layered, stepped pages are created by varying the width of each page.

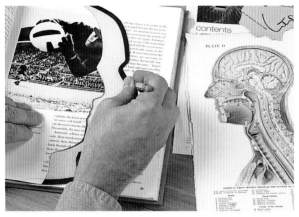

• The pages are colored with acrylics or decorative paper. The eye image on the left is an illustration for the covered-over text. I masked the edges of the illustration with low-tack painter's tape to protect it as I painted the page.

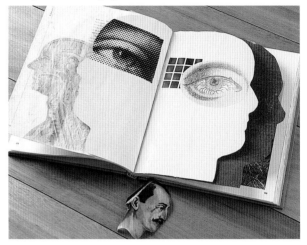

• Here's the finished spread of pages. Additional imagery and lettering completed the spread.

Shaping Books

Don't like the shape of your book? Books with unique shapes appeal to many artists. Children's board books are easily cut into shapes.

• Glue a photocopy of a shape directly on the book's cover. Cut out the shape with a sharp craft knife one layer at a time. A small, electric jigsaw will cut through the entire stack of pages easily and smoothly.

The bus book became the handbook.

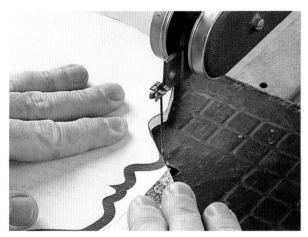

This "handbook" of proverbs and popular sayings was cut from a child's board book. It's a work in progress, as you can see from the unaltered pages inside.

TERRY TAYLOR, *Adage Handbook*, 2003
Paint, gold leaf, wood, plastic, pencil, 5½ x 11½ in. (14 x 29.2 cm)
Photo by Steve Mann

Adding Color to Pages

It's a good idea to experiment with the paper in your book before you begin altering the pages. Some text pages are more absorbent than others. Fluid mediums will wrinkle pages as they dry. The thicker page stock of some books may not need to be strengthened before applying very light coats of wet mediums. It's important to have some idea of how the paper will react to the medium you intend to use.

Dry mediums—colored pencils, crayons, chalks, or stamping inks—can be applied directly to both single or strengthened pages to provide color.

• If you wish to preserve text or imagery on the page, you'll need to mask those areas (see page 55). To completely obscure text and imagery on the page, cover strengthened pages with one or two coats of gesso. Then use any appropriate medium you wish to add color to your pages. For best results, apply wet mediums (paints and inks) to strengthened page stacks or heavy page stock. Be sure to slip a sheet of waxed paper behind your page to protect the pages underneath.

• Shorten the drying time of single coats of paint, fluid inks, or stamping inks by using a hair dryer. Make sure the page is bone dry before you attempt to glue anything to it.

• Adding paper to pages is also an excellent way to add both color and strength to pages at the same time. Thin decorative papers—tissue papers, Oriental papers, or dress patterns—work well. Cut two pieces of paper to your page size or slightly larger. Spread a thin layer of acrylic medium on a single page. Lay the decorative paper on the page and burnish it with a bone folder. Repeat this process on the back of the page. Otherwise, the page will warp and wrinkle. Use waxed paper to protect the page and press it flat overnight.

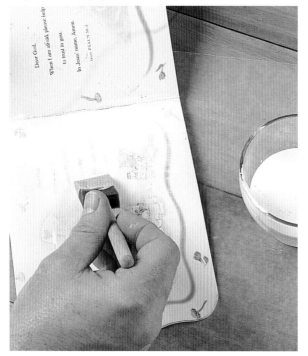

• In the example on the left, Susan McBride painted simple, graphic designs on a cover. Her title is printed on a paper bookplate glued to the cover. The brass charms are sewn to the cover to allow them to move.

Working on the Cover

The cover of your altered book is just as important as the inside. It invites the viewer in, and clues the viewer on what's to come. Use any and all techniques you're comfortable working with to alter the cover of your book. Some artists leave the cover as is, especially if the cover may have been the springboard for the altered pages that follow. Other artists use the cover as another substrate to work on. No matter what your approach, you can (and people do) judge a book by its cover.

• Prepare a hardbound cover with one or more coats of gesso. The gesso will obscure any illustration and prepares the surface for paints. You can mask portions of your cover as desired.

• Tracy Roos created a digital transparency, covered the book with a textured paper, and stitched the transparency to the cover with wire. The spine of her book was embellished further with small, jeweled metal charms.

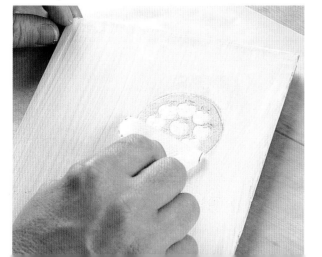

Basic Technique Projects

These first six projects work together to illustrate some basic techniques used to alter books. I purchased a set of travel books from the Salvation Army thrift store in town. The books were the same size, had loads of color photographs, thick page stock, and sturdy binding. Then I recruited designers, assigned each a specific technique, and set a limited time frame for completion. I asked them to create a two-page spread and sent each designer the following description of the theme I'd chosen to work with.

Some of the designers requested that they work in a specific book—Sheila Petruccelli wanted Spain and Tracy Roos, Greece. Not every designer created simply a single page-spread. Some designers returned their books with the covers embellished and additional page spreads created. The pages that follow show a variety of working styles and interpretations of the theme. They'll also give you an idea of the variety you can expect to see if you participate in a round robin (see page 51). The directions are meant to guide and inspire you to create your own pages, not to tell you how to duplicate the work.

PERSONAL MYTHS

Do you see yourself as Atlas carrying the weight of the world (represented by aging parents or the "baggage" of a failed relationship)? Is someone you know a Leda being courted by the swan (aren't we all deceived by disguises)? Does a myth speak to you and some aspect of your life (be it Medusa, Tristan and Isolde, Krishna, the Raven, Osiris, Jonah, Minerva, Merlin, or the Southern Belle)?

Interpret the personal myth theme in your own way on your pages.

Pages from Susan McBride's
A Myth of Romance (pages 48-50)

The heartbreaker knew she would break hearts.

Painting and Drawing on Pages

"Is romance a manufactured idea? Over several pages I imagine the course of romance between a man and woman. The birth of their daughter—The Heartbreaker—explores what happens when you hang such a nickname on a little girl. Is romance a myth?"

Susan McBride, DESIGNER

MATERIALS   Acrylic paint • Gesso • Graphite • Hand-carved rubber-stamp images
Computer printed text • Acrylic medium

1. Susan strengthened the pages and gave them a coat of gesso (see page 36). She masked off some of the original illustrations and text (see page 55).

2. She painted pages with acrylics and drew on them with graphite. Susan used hand-carved rubber stamps to create imagery in a different style from her drawing. She stamped the images onto paper and adhered them to the pages with medium.

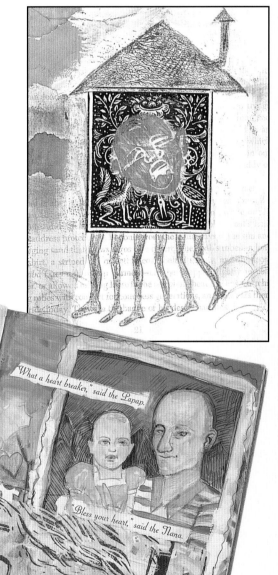

The heartbreaker had an imaginary friend.

Jesus showed his burning heart at Grandmother's house and his eyes followed the heartbreaker where ever she went.

She considered the convent.

How to Carve a Rubber Stamp

- Purchase soft plastic erasers or printing blocks.
- Draw directly on the block with pencil or trace an image on the block using a pencil and carbon paper.
- Use linoleum carving tools to carve away areas you don't wish to print.
- While you are carving, periodically ink the stamp and test print it on paper. This will help you see what additional portions you need to carve away.

3. The additional bucolic imagery was created with laser prints on paper, then collaged them to the pages with medium.

4. Susan chose the text style—a 1960s display type face—to reflect on the false promises of advertising. She composed it on a computer, laser printed it on paper, and adhered it with acrylic medium.

What's a Round Robin?

Tired of working in a vacuum? Would you enjoy collaborating and interacting with like-minded souls on an altered book? If so, a round robin is just the sort of activity you're looking for.

In a round robin game, each player plays every player in the group at least once. In an altered book round robin, each person alters one or more pages. You can circulate one book or several books among the artists. Working with a group is part of the charm of the round robin. You'll get to look at and learn from the work of others as the books make their rounds. And don't fret, if you send out a book to start a round robin it eventually returns to you!

Who's in Charge?

From the playground to the office, every group activity is directed by someone. If you're working with a small group of friends or like-minded artists in your town, decisions on theme, time span, and the do's and don'ts for the round robin often are decided with face-to-face discussion. Altered book groups on the Internet depend on a host to initiate and oversee the process, keeping tabs on the exchange of books and many other details. You'll find lengthy and detailed postings of host duties on altered book websites.

Choosing a Theme

The theme for a round robin may be chosen by group consensus, but hosts usually determine the theme. Perhaps it's a theme they're already working on, and they want to invite the participation of other artists. Colors, stories, single words, events, book content, emotions, techniques, book shape, and whim inspire themes.

Etiquette

First and foremost, respect the creative work of the other participants. Treat their work as you'd like yours to be treated. Pay attention to the established time frames. Adhere to the specific rules—for materials, techniques, or theme—when you're working. If you're mailing a book to a group member, take special care when you pack the book for transit.

Sign Your Work

Sign your individual pages. In addition, a portion of the book is usually set aside for members of the group to add contact information or a personal statement.

They smile in your face…

Niche and Page Extension

"My mother tried diligently to turn me into a Southern Belle, but without success. One of my mother's gloves, a copy of a hand tinted photo of my mother as a toddler, a charm from my debutant days in Alabama, and costume jewelry from my sorority days are all used in this spread. The antebellum house—Multiflora—is the one my mother grew up in. The smiling illustration of the gloved woman (I added the knife charm) reminded me of those belles who smile in your face while preparing to stab you in the back. I'm not sure how the spread ended up becoming a triptych, and I feel it's still a work in progress."

Katie Metheny, DESIGNER

MATERIALS Watercolor paper • Images • Acrylic paint • Lace • Costume jewelry
Found objects • Gel medium • Fibers • Muslin • Ink jet photo paper • Eyelets

1. Katie created a niche for her glove at the back of the book (see page 39). Then she adhered lace to the niche background to create texture and painted it with acrylic paint.

2. She stained a large sheet of watercolor paper with light washes of acrylic paint.

Designer Tip

If you don't want to use acrylic paint washes, brush on a wash of coffee or strong black tea. Herbal teas and green teas will tint the paper differently from black teas. Experiment with different types of tea for different effects. Sprinkle coffee grounds on paper washed with coffee to create a speckled look.

3. Katie measured the height and width of the opened book spread, adding approximately one inch (2.54 cm) to the width. She cut the stained paper to these measurements, then marked and cut out the niche shape on the paper.

4. She glued the flat collage elements—color photocopies, ink-jet printed muslin, magazine cutouts—to the paper, then set a few eyelets on the paper and attached a few elements with thread. She glued the sheet to the book with gel medium and allowed the medium to dry completely before she added the dimensional elements.

5. As she worked on the two-page spread, Katie was inspired to extend it. She set eyelets on one edge of the watercolor paper she had glued to the book (see page 99). She cut a single-page size piece of watercolor and added eyelets to one side. After embellishing the page, Katie joined the two pages with ribbon lacing.

Persephone

PERSEPHONE WAS ABDUCTED BY HADES AND MADE QUEEN OF THE UNDERWORLD DEMETER, GODDESS OF THE HARVEST, GRIEVED ENDLESSLY FOR HER LOST DAUGHTER AND NO CROPS WOULD GROW ON EARTH FEARING THE END OF HUMANKIND, HADES AGREED TO RELEASE PERSEPHONE, BUT BECAUSE SHE HAD EATEN THREE SEEDS OF A POMEGRANATE SHE MUST RETURN TO THE UNDERWORLD EACH YEAR FOR THREE MONTHS.

BEWARE

Pomegranate

MORAL OF THE STORY—
TEMPTATION AND FOOD
WERE A PROBLEM WAY
BEFORE EVE!

Liquid polymer clay transfer

Polymer Clay Embellishments

"The myth of Persephone appeals to me for several different reasons. As a mother of one daughter, I understand the bond between Demeter, mother of Persephone, and her child. It is a myth of hope, reminding us that 'this too shall pass.' Winter gives way to spring. Life goes on. On a less serious note, I have to laugh at the fact that food was getting women in trouble long before Eve ate the apple."

Lynn B. Krucke, DESIGNER

MATERIALS Ink pads • Masking tape • Decorative papers • Skeleton leaf • Rubber stamps Alphabet stickers • Metal frame • Eyelets • Polymer clay • Liquid polymer clay Metallic powdered mica pigments

1. Lynn cut out a shallow niche to hold a polymer clay embellishment she planned to create for the spread.

2. Before adding the color background to the pages, Lynn chose to mask several words in the printed text that related to her theme. For example, three, for the three seeds of a pomegranate, and unfavorable weather, for the winter season caused by Persephone's descent into the underworld. She used masking tape to cover words and other areas on the pages before adding color with ink pads.

Designer Tip

• Trim strips of masking tape or low-tack painter's tape to size to cover individual words or lines of type.

• To prevent tape from damaging the page when removed, press it lightly to your clothing a few times before placing it on your book. The fibers (and all that lint) that the tape picked up will make it a lot less sticky.

• To mask illustrations, photos, or large areas, cut a piece of waxed paper slightly smaller than the area you wish to cover. Tape the waxed paper in place.

3. Lynn added text to the pages with rubber stamps, alphabet stickers, and computer-generated text printed on translucent vellum. She created imagery with rubber stamps, photo copies, and a liquid polymer transfer.

How to Make a Liquid Polymer Transfer

• Use a toner-based color copy of your image or print your image on matte photo paper with an inkjet printer.

• Spread a thin layer of liquid polymer clay on the image. The flexibility and translucency of the transfer are determined by the amount of clay used.

• Bake the image according to the manufacturer's guidelines.

• Soak the baked image in water. Remove the paper by rubbing back and forth with your fingertips, rolling away the soaked paper. Allow the piece to dry, then look for fuzzy white areas. Moisten those spots and rub again until no paper remains.

• Trim the image and mount to page as desired.

4. Lynn created dimensional elements for the page with polymer clay. She pressed textured rubber stamps into unbaked black clay, then rubbed metallic powders to highlight the textured clay. The individual shapes were cut out, and the clay was baked according to the manufacturer's instructions.

5. She glued dimensional elements to the page or attached them with eyelets (see page 99).

Stamped and Collaged Pages

"Atlas Is a Woman" reflects my belief that women support the world through a myriad of tasks done with loving hands. I start with a basic plan or concept, but for the most part making art is an intuitive process for me. Some of the positioning of the elements here was purely by trial and error in order to achieve the balance and depth I desired. By adding subsequent layers I achieved my goal of subtle complexity. At first glance, this piece appears calm and simple but, as in life, much is going on underneath and around that we are not aware of until we slow down and look closely."

Barbara Matthiessen, DESIGNER

MATERIALS   Acrylic paint • Clear embossing ink • Rubber stamps with circle motifs
Pearl powders • Acrylic medium • Text paper • Pigment inks • Rubber stamps
Alphabet stamps • Metallic crayons • Heat gun • Card stock • Metallic gel pen • Metallic marker

1. Barbara strengthened her pages to prepare them for acrylic paint (see page 36).

2. She inked rubber stamps with clear embossing ink and randomly stamped over the painted background. Then Barbara dusted the stamped images with small amounts pearl powder.

3. Barbara created text by clipping words from magazines, junk mail, and other sources. She chose varied sizes of type and fonts to add interest to her composition. She adhered the letters with acrylic medium. To add color to the decoupaged words, Barbara dabbed a pigment ink pad over them, then softly blended the ink with a paintbrush.

4. She used photocopies of earth and globe imagery, then added more imagery to these cut shapes with rubber stamps. All imagery was adhered to the pages with acrylic medium.

5. Barbara stamped "Atlas Is a Woman" onto a text page from an old encyclopedia. By chance (or design), it came from the entry on feminism.

6. To mimic the look of encaustic painting, she added coats of colored wax that give a subtle sheen and add depth to areas of the page.

Faux Encaustic Painting

Practice this technique on scrap paper before working on your page spread.

- Remove the paper label from a wax crayon.
- Using tweezers or tongs, hold the end of the crayon about one inch away from the end of a heat gun. Melt the end of the crayon and allow a few drops to drip onto the page. After a few drops of wax are on the page, set the crayon aside.
- Hold the heat gun above the drops of wax, moving it from side to side. The heat will spread the wax on the page. Don't allow the heat gun to point at one area for too long a time.
- Add a second color, if desired. Use the heat gun to blend the colors.
- Build thicker layers of colored wax, if desired.

7. Barbara used clip art images of a butterfly and hands copied onto card stock, which she cut out and adhered to the pages with medium.

Cut-and-Folded Pages

"The idea of myth as an archetypal story, rather than an untruth, captured my imagination. The myth of the divine feminine is a theme I've been working with for some time, and I've always loved the form of a medieval triptych. After deciding to mimic a triptych with my layout, the rest of the choices were made when I received the book on Spain. Spanish culture influenced my bold color palette, imagery, and text."

Sheila Petruccelli, DESIGNER

MATERIALS   Acrylic paints • Alphabet stamps • Card stock • Gel medium
Lace • Envelopes • Fibers • Gold leaf

1. Sheila used eight pages to create this spread.

2. She painted two background pages with red acrylic. Then she used a rubber stamp alphabet and silver acrylic paint to stamp the prayer text on the pages.

3. She created the tags with white card stock. Images of the Madonna and fibers decorate the cards. Sheila wanted to insert the tags into pockets, rather than attaching them to pages.

How to Create Pockets for Tags

- Place each tag on the back of your page. Decide how much of the tag you want to peek out from the pocket.
- Trace around each tag.
- Adhere narrow double-sided tape slightly outside the traced lines.
- Run a line of glue around the outer edge of the page. Be certain you avoid the opening end of the pocket.
- Adhere the page to the page behind.

4. Sheila cut the next pages diagonally. She glued black lace on the front side and trimmed it; then painted the back side with black acrylic. She glued envelopes to the back of each page and filled them with prayer cards, images, and faux currency.

5. The cut pages in the center spread she covered with a thin, transparent paper and patterned tissue. Sheila photocopied the image and hand colored it with pencils. She cut the image in half and each half was glued to a page. Then she sealed the image with a coat of gel medium and sprinkled it with gold leaf while the medium was still wet.

6. Sheila machine stitched red lace onto a length of black lace then glued the layered strip of lace to the edges of the book's cover.

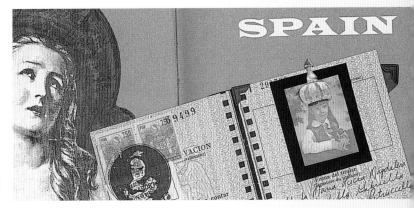

The altered photo is a childhood school portrait of the artist.

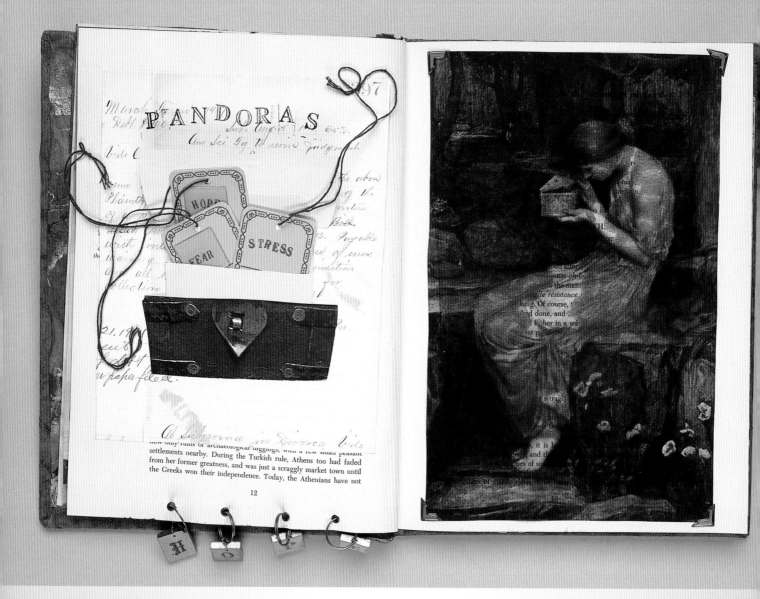

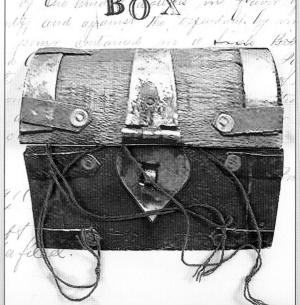

Creating Digital Imagery for Pages

"In my studio I'm always missing something. I can't find the glue, scissors, and where the heck did that photo go? With digital collage, nothing gets lost; everything is at your fingertips with no sticky glue fingers or scraps of paper to pick up afterward. Computer programs are easy to use, and with the affordable, great quality scanners and printers available today, it's easy to print out little masterpieces every day."

Tracy Roos, DESIGNER

MATERIALS   Computer • Printer • Scanner • Card stock • Ink-jet transparency
Alphabet stamps • Photographs • Library card pocket • Decorative papers

1. Tracy glued card stock printed with calligraphy on the page as a background. She added text to the page with a rubber stamp alphabet.

2. Next, she created a moveable pocket—for Pandora's box—that opened and closed on the page. She did it by scanning a photograph of an old chest, sizing the image, and printing it on matte photo paper.

How to Make a Moveable Pocket
- Cut your image in half.
- Fold down the top edge of the library card pocket.
- Glue the pocket to the page.
- Glue the top half of the image to the folded edge. Align the bottom half of the image with the top half, and glue it in place on the pocket.

3. Tracy created small tags and rubber-stamped them with words describing the contents of the chest. She slipped the tags into the library pocket.

4. She scanned the image of Pandora on the facing page and printed onto an ink-jet transparency. Tracy adhered a piece of Asian paper decorated with

gold leaf to the page, then glued the transparency on top of it. Finally, she added faux photo corners to the page.

5. Tracy set eyelets along the bottom edge of one page, and attached jewelry findings to wooden letter tiles and secured them to the page with split-rings.

The legend of Pandora is the God Hephaistos created a woman of the earth and named her Pandora. The Goddesses of Olympus blessed her with great beauty and allure. Then draped her with fine clothing. The only flaw this woman had was her extreme curiosity. The Gods gifted her to Prometheus' brother Epimetheus. He fell in love with her and promptly married her. The Gods then gave the happy couple a lovely box as a wedding present. They were warned to never open this box, and it would bring them good fortune. Months passed and the mysterious box weighed heavily on Pandora mind.

Digital imagery printed on acetate transparency

PERSONAL myths

Creating a Cover

"The myth of Icarus appeals to me as a cautionary tale—our rise and inevitable fall whether flying on beautiful, foolish wings (thank you, Joni Mitchell) or climbing the corporate ladder. As I thought about the cover, I searched for proverbs about striving for success. I typed Icarus into my search engine and rediscovered the poems of William Carlos Williams and W.H. Auden that were inspired by Pieter Brueghel's (1525–1569) Landscape with the Fall of Icarus. I added those elements to the inside of the cover."

Terry Taylor, DESIGNER

MATERIALS   Gesso • Acrylic paint • Water slide decal • Transparency acetate • Metal foil
Beads • Rubber stamp alphabet • Metal eyelet letters • Decorative paper • Matte medium • Acrylic varnish

1. I prepared the surface of the cover with gesso (page 45) and painted it with acrylics. I wanted to mimic the uneven color of the sky, so I lightly sanded the cover after it was painted.

2. The graph and chart I drew with permanent ink on the painted surface.

3. I collaged vintage imagery on the cover. The clip-art image of the businessman was created on a water slide decal (see page 18).

4. I was unsure how to create the sun image I had in mind for the cover. A little meditative rummaging (page 25) allowed me to find a magazine image of a blue framed mirror that inspired my sun.

5. I envisioned a window where I could suspend a single feather. To make one of the window panes, I created a collage using an advertisement and a photocopy of *Icarus* by Henri Matisse (1869–1954). I cut Icarus out of black paper, laid it on the advertisement, and made a color transparency of the collage at the copy shop.

How to Create a Two-Sided Window

• Trace the shape of your window on the cover.

• I have a small jigsaw that I used to cut out the traced shape. You can also cut out the shape with a sharp craft knife. If you use a craft knife, don't try to cut through in one stroke. Cut through the cover a little bit at a time.

• Cut a piece of your photocopied collage on acetate slightly larger than the cutout on the cover. Cut a second shape the same size as the first from clear acetate. If desired, you can simply use two clear panes of acetate for your window.

• Glue the collaged image to the back of the window. Place your object inside, and glue the clear piece of acetate to the front.

6. I covered the edges of the acetate with the cutout image of the blue mirror. I cut out a frame from metal foil, embossed it, and glued it to the cover. Then, I pierced around the window with an awl and stitched beads onto the cover.

7. For the title, I selected metal eyelet letters. Rather than setting the eyelets, I glued them to the cover (see page 99).

Altered Book Projects

Now that you've been introduced to the basic techniques for altering books, here are four more altered book projects using a board book, textbook, vintage salesman's book, and an album for old-fashioned 78 rpm records.

This spit-curled beauty is semiprecious: a little trashy, yet powerfully beautiful, as good costume jewelry should be.

Bee Jeweled

"This small 'jewel' of a book is one volume—O and P—of a child's set of alphabet board books. Still visible, an orange becomes an earring, an owl a queen's companion, and the pig .... "

Susan McBride, DESIGNER

MATERIALS   Gesso • Acrylic paint • Masking tape • Colored pencils • Faux gems
Engagement ring • Vellum • Acrylic medium • Brass stamping • Wire

1. Susan prepared the glossy pages of the book with two or three coats of gesso (see page 44).

2. She gave the cover a base coat of acrylic paint. Then she drilled small holes through the bee's wings and the cover. She used thin wire to sew the bee to the cover. She threaded beads and pearls onto the wire as she sewed on the wings, then twisted the wire on the back of the cover and covered it with tape.

The queen's jewels evoke the cold, icy beauty of precious regal stones.

3. With paint and colored pencils she drew the concentric circles around the bee. Then she glued faux gems to the circles.

4. Susan composed the text on a computer, and printed it out on translucent vellum. She adhered the printed vellum medium. As the medium dried, the vellum wrinkled and took on a weathered look that appealed to her.

5. She used imagery clipped from magazines and decoupaged it on the pages with medium, then added gems and pearls to the pages in keeping with the theme. The gems were glued on; the strands of pearls were wired to the pages.

6. Susan cut through the thick page with a craft knife and created a window for the final two-page spread. She wired a diamond engagement ring to the page that follows.

Look closely at the text: It's a Dear John letter.

Making a M(dr)ess

"Here's an example of a round robin book. The book's subject, making a dress, was illustrated with simple drawings and the paper cover was intact when I found it. I invited editors and art directors—most of whom had never before altered a book—to work in the book. After several pages had been worked on, I asked Suzanne Gernandt, a local fiber artist, to alter the cover and add her own page spread."

Terry Taylor, DESIGNER

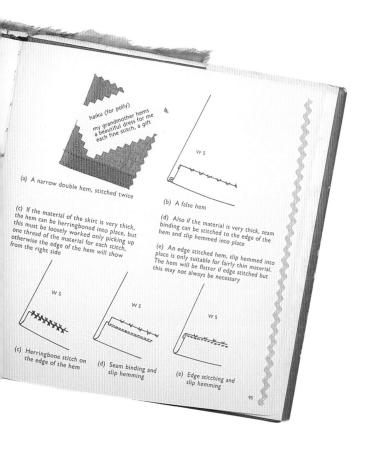

(a) A narrow double hem, stitched twice

(b) A false hem

(c) If the material of the skirt is very thick, the hem can be herringboned into place, but this must be loosely worked only picking up one thread of the material for each stitch, otherwise the edge of the material for the hem will show from the right side

(d) Also if the material is very thick, seam binding can be stitched to the edge of the hem and slip hemmed into place

(e) An edge stitched hem, slip hemmed into place is only suitable for fairly thin material. The hem will be flatter if edge stitched but this may not always be necessary

(c) Herringbone stitch on the edge of the hem

(d) Seam binding and slip hemming

(e) Edge stitching and slip hemming

95

haiku (for polly)

my grandmother hems
a beautiful dress for me
each fine stitch, a gift

1. Many commonly used techniques were employed in making this book: drawing, image transfer, and collage.

2. Susan McBride worked on the title page, using graphite, ink, and gouache. She illustrated the classic cry of woe uttered by anyone who's searching for a special outfit in her closet.

3. Valerie Shrader learned to sew from her grandmother (and won a Betty Crocker award in high school!). She composed a haiku, printed it out on

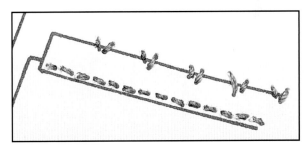

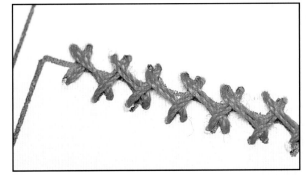

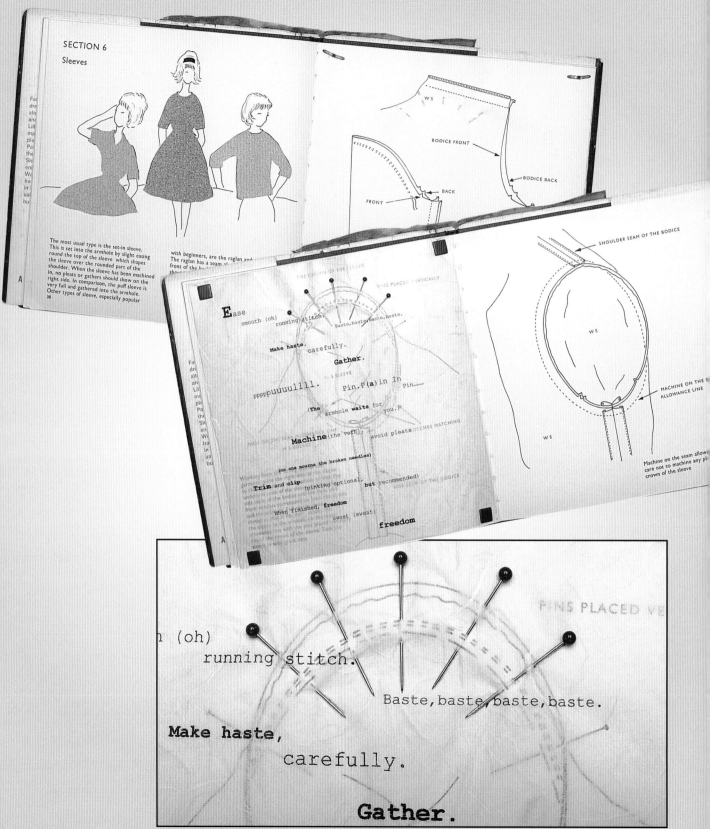

her printer, and attached it to the page. Then she meticulously stitched on top of the stitching illustrations.

4. Megan Kirby traced dress shapes in an illustration, cut them out of sandpaper, and glued them in place. The rough material comments on the strictures of fashion.

5. Jane LaFerla created a found poem with words and phrases she found in the book. She printed the poem onto tissue and attached it to the page with brads and dressmaker's pins.

6. I colored my page with stamping ink, then added a solvent transfer with a photocopy of a corset image. I stamped the words corset and cosset (each brings to mind different aspects of holding) onto the page, and used eyelets to evoke the tyranny of old-fashioned corsets (picture Miss Scarlett being laced up by Mammy).

7. Suzanne Gernandt altered the cover (and the title!) with paint, collage, fabric, and stitching. Her page spread plays off the illustration of body types and comments on the obsession with body type and size in our culture.

A Family Memory Album

"I used photos of actual ancestors, both mine and my husband's. The spoon is a flea market purchase, but I added it for its decorative value and because it's something those ancestors might have used. The floral decorative paper was chosen to evoke a nostalgic feeling."

Jane Reeves, DESIGNER

MATERIALS   Multisleeved record album • Photos • Acrylic paints • Acrylic medium
Decorative papers • Fabric • Lettering materials • Silk flowers

1. Jane selected her photos for the front and back covers, as well as the inside page sleeves. She photocopied the photographs, enlarging or reducing them as needed.

2. To give the illusion of peeling wallpaper and antique upholstery, she composed the background layers with different sizes and shapes of torn decorative paper or fabric. She adhered the shapes with acrylic medium.

3. Jane stained the covers and inside pages with a light coat of acrylic paint thinned with medium. She immediately rubbed the coat of paint with a dampened paper towel to create a washed effect, then let the coated pages and cover dry completely.

4. She glued the images onto the cover and pages with the medium. She cut out frames from decorative paper and glued them into place on the images.

5. Using paper and fabric, Jane cut flower and leaf shapes, arranged them around the framed images, and then glued them in place. To blend them into the background she lightly sponged on the thinned acrylic color. If the color was too dark, she wiped the color with with a dampened paper towel.

6. She used her favorite lettering materials to add words or phrases to the album. Then, bit by bit, she added embellishments such as silk flowers or ribbon without gluing them. When she was satisfied with the composition, she glued them in place with a thick white glue.

Square scrapbook pages fit nicely into the sleeves of this album. Slip collages created with family photos and paper emphemera into the sleeves.

all in the same *chest* size. It is easily seen that the man with the forty-inch chest may have a sixty-inch trunk, a sixty-four-inch or a sixty-eight-inch trunk. A m... a forty-inch chest and a sixty-inch trunk is a... A man who has a sixty-eight-inch trunk and ...rty chest is a slim man, although he is quite... These illustrations show the absolute necessi... ...ting different lengths of trunk in each and ev... ...measurement.

Mr. B... ...man; Mr. Smith a ...all, slim ...th ...forty-inch chest; Brown had a s...ch tru... ...mith had a sixty-eight-inch tru... ...e day, be... oth wore forty-...nch chest suits, ...suits got ... Fig. 3 shows Brown in Smith'... it is all r... ...h the chest but oo long. Fig. 1 ...s Smith in ...n's suit, which s too short. Wh... ...ey traded ... Fig. 2 shows mith, and Fig. 4 ... Brown, ea... his own suit. This shows that *a s... man cannot ... a slim man's uit,* even if the che... ...; the same. ...oper's make touts (large aroun... nd Slims (s...l around)— ight in trunk and righ... chest, and ...ers do so.

SIZE DOES MATTER

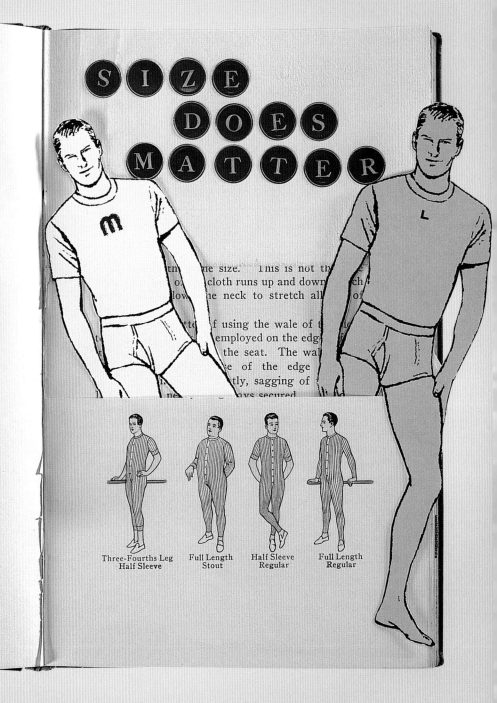

...th... ...e size. This is not th... ...e o... cloth runs up and down... ...ch low... ...e neck to stretch all... ...of ...tt... ...f using the wale of t... ...employed on the edg... ...the seat. The wal... ...e of the edge ...tly, sagging of ...ne... ...ys secured

Three-Fourths Leg Half Sleeve   Full Length Stout   Half Sleeve Regular   Full Length Regular

Tips and Pointers for Underwear Dealers and Their Salesmen

"A friend, who happens to be a rare book dealer, gives me odd volumes he thinks I'll be drawn to with only one stricture: 'You can do what you want with this book.' The man knows my penchant for cutting and pasting all too well. Instead of sitting on my shelf untouched, this volume is now a work in progress."

Terry Taylor, DESIGNER

MATERIALS   Milagro or charm • Tags • Measuring tape • Alphabet stamps • Eyelets • Card stock • Vintage imagery

1. First, I read the book cover to cover. Published in 1923, it's a fascinating peek into a salesman's world in the early part of the century. Photographs of arcane knitting machinery, illustrations of wool and cotton, and tips on how to sell perfectly fitted underwear became springboards for working on the book.

2. I rummaged through my piles (not files!) of imagery for inspiration but found few things that appealed to me. I envisioned a certain kind of

imagery but didn't have it. Then it hit me: I wanted an old Sears Roebuck catalog. With a few clicks of my computer mouse, and few key words typed in, I placed a bid on a catalog. A week later I had a gold mine of illustrations to use for this and future projects.

3. As I worked on the project, I was drawn again and again to the section of the book describing the "selling points" tags that were attached to a sales-

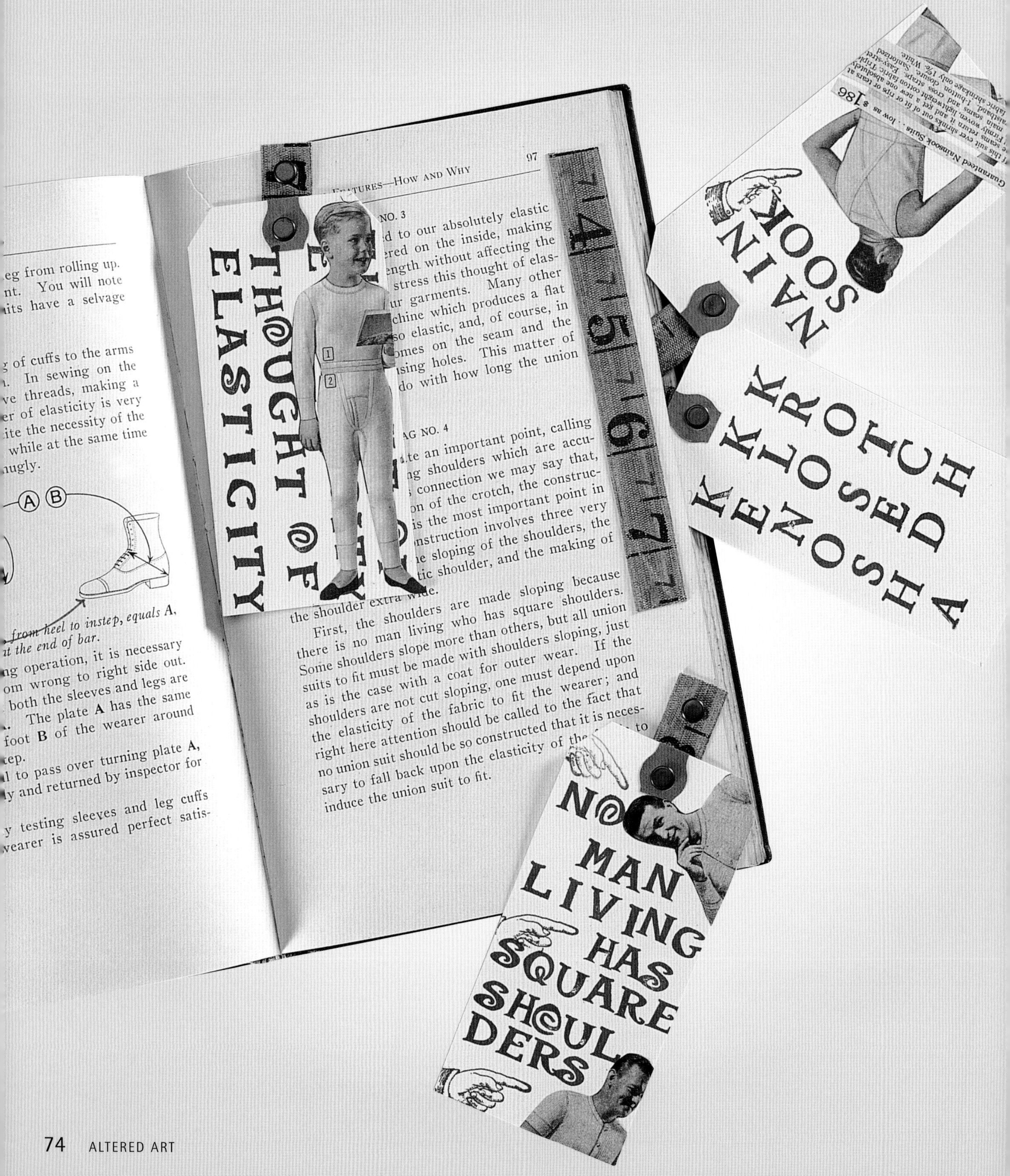

eg from rolling up.
nt.   You will note
its have a selvage

g of cuffs to the arms
. In sewing on the
ve threads, making a
er of elasticity is very
te the necessity of the
while at the same time
ugly.

(A) (B)

from heel to instep, equals A,
t the end of bar.
ng operation, it is necessary
om wrong to right side out.
both the sleeves and legs are
.   The plate A has the same
foot B of the wearer around
ep.
l to pass over turning plate A,
y and returned by inspector for

y testing sleeves and leg cuffs
wearer is assured perfect satis-

THOUGHT OF ELASTICITY

NO. 3
d to our absolutely elastic
ered on the inside, making
ength without affecting the
stress this thought of elas-
ur garments.   Many other
chine which produces a flat
so elastic, and, of course, in
omes on the seam and the
sing holes.   This matter of
do with how long the union

AG NO. 4
te an important point, calling
g shoulders which are accu-
connection we may say that,
on of the crotch, the construc-
is the most important point in
construction involves three very
sloping of the shoulders, the
tic shoulder, and the making of
the shoulder extra wide.

First, the shoulders are made sloping because
there is no man living who has square shoulders.
Some shoulders slope more than others, but all union
suits to fit must be made with shoulders sloping, just
as is the case with a coat for outer wear. If the
shoulders are not cut sloping, one must depend upon
the elasticity of the fabric to fit the wearer; and
right here attention should be called to the fact that
no union suit should be so constructed that it is necessary to fall back upon the elasticity of the   to
induce the union suit to fit.

74 75 76 77

NAIN SOOK

KROTCH KLOSED A HSOZSH

186

NO MAN LIVING HAS SQUARE SHOULDERS

man's sample of underwear. (Alas, it did not come with the book. If you find one, please let me know!) I collaged imagery on tags and rubber-stamped phrases and words from the book's text.

The book had a detailed description of the importance of measuring for a perfect fit. I wanted to attach the tags with lengths of measuring tape, but the bright yellow plastic tapes I found just didn't work. Again, with a few clicks of my mouse, I found a vintage tape. I used eyelets to attach the tags to the pages (see page 99).

4. I created a simple pocket by cutting a page in half and then ran a line of glue along two edges. I added text with stickers and transfer lettering. The clip art paper dolls I copied onto card stock, cut out, and slipped into the pocket.

5. The illustration of the grades of wool on a sheep in the book brought to mind similar illustrations of meat cuts in cookbooks. I found my illustrations in a dictionary and an old anatomy text. I like to use the original material and not photocopies whenever possible.

6. I pondered altering the cover for a very long time. The embossed gold medallion, elaborately embossed text, and faux leather binding really needed no embellishment. One day I was sorting through a small assortment of milagros looking for something for another project. I looked at the brass leg, looked at the book sitting on my work table, and reached for the glue. I live for those moments of serendipity!

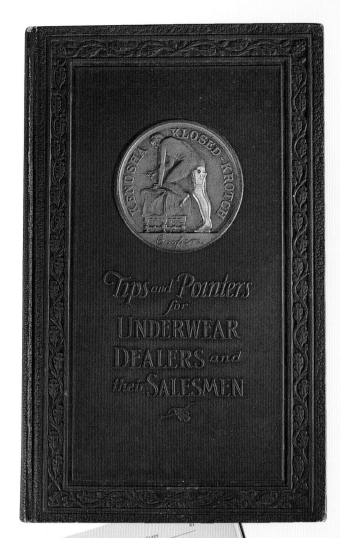

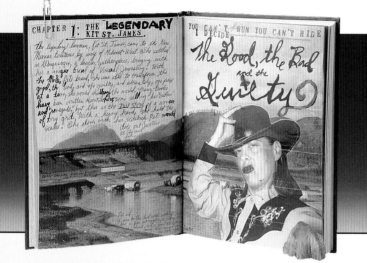

JULIANA COLES, *The Chronicles of Kit St. James*, 2003-work in progress
Time-Life book from the series *The Old West*, digital photos, India ink,
china marker, tape, 8½ x 11 x ¾ in. (21.6 x 27.9 x 1.9 cm)
Photos by Pat Berrett

*I have a Wild West alter ego I named Kit St. James;
for this project I chose to bring her to life. I dressed up like
a cowgirl and took photos of myself with my digital
camera to fit into the scenes of the pages already there.*

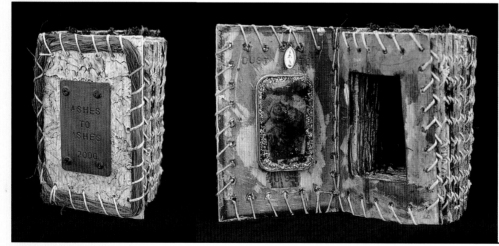

DAWN WILSON, *Ashes to Ashes*, 2003
Discarded book, acrylic paint, ink, shoe polish, dried iris leaves; laminated, tied, 7¾ x 5
x 2¾ in. (19.7 x 12.7 x 6.9 cm)
Photos by artist

*This book was a therapeutic release of my father's passing of cancer.
The inside front cover has an Altoid tin cover with the funeral card,
on acetate, superimposed over his baby picture. Each page has
the words from the funeral service found in the Book of
Common Prayer. The inside back cover is an Altoid tin filled
with my father's trinkets, and an acetate of him in his adult years.*

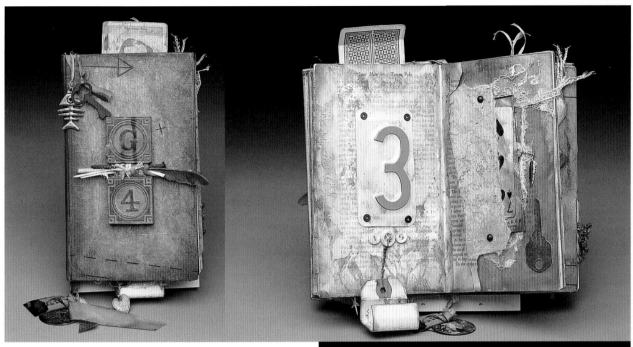

Clockwise from left:

CAROL OWEN, *Mariposa*, 2003
Altered book, acrylic paint, found objects,
7¹/2 x 4¹/2 x 2 in. (19 x 11.4 x 5 cm)
Photo by Seth Tice-Lewis

Three, 2003
Altered book, acrylic paint, found objects,
7¹/2 x 8¹/4 x 1³/4 in. (19 x 21 x 4.4 cm)
Photo by Seth Tice-Lewis

Untitled, 2003
Altered book, paint, found objects,
7¹/2 x 8¹/4 x ¹/2 in. (19 x 21 x 1.3 cm)
Photos by Seth Tice-Lewis

PATRICIA CHAPMAN, *One Must Never*, 2002
Emily Post etiquette book, forks, metal frame, constructed
box, 17½ x 12⅝ x 4½ in. (44.5 x 32.1 x 11.4 cm)
Collection of Antonia Robertson
Photos by artist

JAYE WHITWORTH, *My Life's an Open Book with Bookmark "Her
White Sheets of Paper on Fire,"* 2002
Plywood panel, gesso, paint, pencil, nails, found objects,
12 x 12 x ½ in. (30.5 x 30.5 x 1.3 cm)
Photo by William Livingston

*One of my prevailing concerns is with the passage of
time–not in its grander conceptions but rather as I experience it in its smallest, most ordinary increments. I try to
evoke, through calligraphic marks (circles, letters, and
scribbles), the rhythm and patterns of ruminative thought
that characterize my awareness as a being moving
through time. Much of my work suggests maps, diaries,
notebooks and calendars–things we use to chart and mark
an individual course within a larger flow
of time and space.*

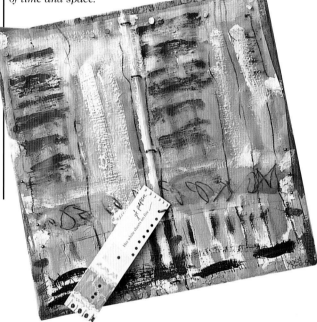

JAYE WHITWORTH,
One Thing Leads to Another, 2002
Hardbound book, found materials, paint,
ink, pencil, tape,
8 x 5½ x 5½ in. (20.3 x 14 x 14 cm)
Photo by William Livingston

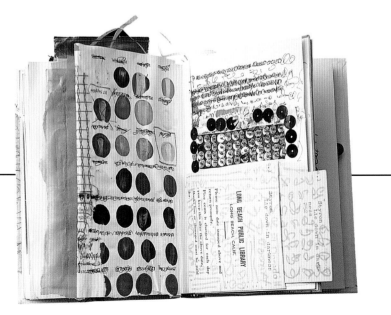

DORIT ELISHA, *Tic-Tag-Toe: Documenting the Life of a Family Through Tags*, 2003
Card pocket wall panel, tags, tickets,
19 x 6 x 1 in. (48.3 x 15.2 x 2.5 cm)
Photo by Dotti Cichon

JUDY WATT *MeMeMe*, 2003 (from ABC Round Robin)
Altered book pages, acrylic paint, metallic pen, photo collage
printed on tissue paper, 9 x 11 in. (22.9 x 27.9 cm)
Photo by artist

Astrology. As Above, So Below, 2003
(from ABC Round Robin)
Altered book pages, acrylic paint, rubber stamping, collage,
plastic mesh, handmade papers, 9 x 11 in. (22.9 x 27.9 cm)
Photo by artist

Basics

Creating a work of art inside a box appeals to many artists. Boxes speak to us on many levels. Is it because we use them to store personal treasure? Delight in unwrapping gifts? Or receive sweets in fancifully decorated tins? Do boxes remind us of shrines or niches in holy places? Or do they invite us to create our own little worlds in three dimensions?

The most widely recognized and slavishly imitated works of art in boxes were created by Joseph Cornell (page 11). Cornell seldom used ready-made boxes. Instead, he meticulously handcrafted boxes that opened and closed so the owners could remove the moveable items inside. The aged appearance of many of his boxes was achieved with a variety of techniques, one of which included baking them in his kitchen oven!

We rarely make our own boxes these days. Instead, we use ready-made boxes to contain assemblages—essentially three dimensional collages—of found objects or objects specifically created for the work. Once you start looking, you'll be amazed by the variety of boxes we have to choose from: craft boxes, matchboxes, antique boxes, and cigar boxes, to name just a few. Brightly lithographed tins and the variously shaped and embossed candy tins in the grocery store checkout line are also available for your use. I've tried many different mints and candies simply to add to my stash of boxes.

BOX BASICS

Working with three-dimensional elements placed inside a box poses two creative challenges: how to change the surface of the box and how to attach elements placed inside or on the box.

Changing the Surface

Use any craft technique you can think of to transform a box's surface. Painting techniques and decoupage are quick and easy. Adhere paper or fabric to the surface of a box with acrylic mediums. Glue mosaic or mirror tiles to a box. The possibilities are endless.

Metal boxes (especially those ubiquitous mint tins) are especially popular with artists and crafters. You can cover the metal surfaces with a variety of mediums, from paper to paint. Metal surfaces can also be changed to reveal the base metal under the paint.

Paint strippers will remove paint. Choose your paint stripper wisely—some are more caustic than others. Be sure to read the manufacturer's directions for the particular stripper you're using. Cover your work surfaces, make sure there's adequate ventilation in your work space, and wear protective gloves. Eye protection and breathing masks may be required as well.

✳ **Designer Tip**

I rust a metal object the old-fashioned way when I don't have an immediate use for it. I leave the object outdoors for this treatment. To speed nature's progress, I fill a spray bottle with cider vinegar and mist the metal. Sometimes I sprinkle coarse or fine salt on the dampened metal to achieve a more pitted effect. Every few days or so I spray the metal. Over time, the acidic vinegar combined with the open air rusts the metal. This is not the quick and easy process that you achieve with commercial solutions, but I find it satisfying nonetheless.

Use a sanding sponge to abrade the paint. You can take off as much or as little as you wish. Sanding also gives bare metal a brushed look. You can take the brushed look of metal even further by scrubbing the bare surface with a circular motion with household scouring pads.

Place your tins in the fireplace or on the barbecue coals (after the main course is cooked, of course) to burn the paint and age the metal.

Burned, stripped, and sanded tins

You can change the color of bare metal itself with a variety of chemical solutions. Darken or tarnish the metal with oxidizing agents, such as liver of sulphur and chemicals for blackening silver, brass, and copper. You'll find these oxidizing agents at most bead stores. You can create patinas—rust or verdigris—with chemical solutions purchased in craft stores. Read the manufacturer's instructions before using any of these solutions.

• Wearing protective gloves, simply brush the metal surfaces with the chemical solution you've purchased. Changes in the color of the metal are almost instantaneous.

Adding Elements

There are no true, hard-and-fast rules for adding elements to boxes. Elements can be attached (or not) in various ways. Many of Joseph Cornell's boxes have moving objects (rings, balls, or papers) in combination with fixed objects (see page 11). You may wish to include moveable objects in your boxes.

Attaching elements to metal boxes can be achieved in three ways: gluing, soldering, or riveting. You can even seemingly suspend objects in air!

Gluing

Reading the section on glues and adhesives (page 31) will give you some information about the suggested uses for different types of glue. You'll need to consider what you want to attach as well as what you're attaching it to. You'll also need to consider the weight of the object. Is it heavy or light? Will the adhesive you've chosen hold the object in place? Do you want a permanent attachment? More than likely you already know the working properties of most glues and have your own particular favorites for different jobs.

Soldering

I mention soldering as an option when working with metal, but it presents certain problems (heat will char painted metal surfaces) and requires skills that aren't used in the projects in this book. Opting to use a cold connection, such as riveting or wiring, is a way to avoid marring painted metal. If your metal isn't painted and you have experience with a soldering iron or torch, then use those skills.

Riveting

By riveting elements to boxes with eyelets you can create the appearance of real metalwork. You'll find many colors, shapes, and types of eyelets in craft stores, all of which can be used to mimic the appearance of rivets. And they're so easy to use.

• Mark where you want to place a rivet. Use an awl or a center punch to make a dimple in the metal.

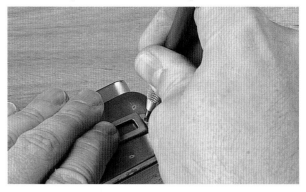

• Drill a hole the same size as your eyelet's stem in both the box and the piece you wish to attach.

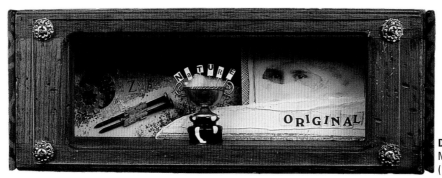

DEBORAH HAYNER, *Original Nature*, 1999
Mixed media, 4½ x 11½ x 4¼ in.
(11.4 x 29.2 x 10.8 cm)

• Hold the drilled pieces with the eyelet inserted and turn over the assembly. Use a hammer and setting tool to spread the stem of the eyelet.

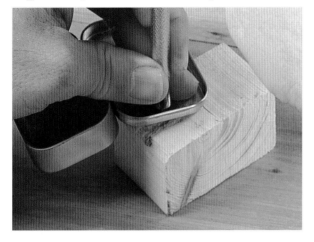

✳ Designer Tip
When working with a metal box, you'll find it useful to work on a small block of wood that fits inside the box. Use it to support the metal when you drill your holes or set the eyelet.

LYNN WHIPPLE, *Gift of the Matriarch*, 2002
Mixed media assemblage, 30 x 40 in. (76 x 102 cm)
Photo by Randall Smith

Suspending Objects

Don't limit yourself to simply gluing objects to a box surface. You can float or suspend objects, too. It may take a little longer to accomplish, but the results are often very effective.

Different types of supports can be created to suspend objects in boxes. Think about material and weight as you consider which objects to suspend. I suspended acrylic sheet using thin strips of wood to hold the sheet above the surface (page 85); Lynn Whipple hung a whimsical figure on wire (page 91).

In other projects, I've drilled holes in the back of the box and impaled objects on nails, screws, and dowels to float them, seemingly unsupported, in midair.

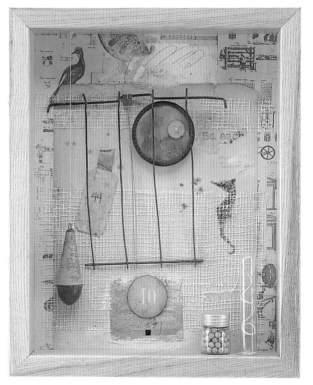

DEBORAH HAYNER, *Ariadne's Sea Saw Mambo*, 2001
Mixed media, 10¾ x 9 x 2 in. (27.3 x 22.9 x 5 cm)

La Palina

"Like Rome, this cigar box shrine wasn't built in a day. The different elements in the box were found and brought together over a period of several months. Most of my work develops over long periods of time as I find pieces (or perhaps they find me!) to incorporate. Then I work in stages, letting things sit until I decide exactly how I want to assemble the piece."

Terry Taylor, DESIGNER

MATERIALS   Cigar box • Water slide transfer paper • Acrylic sheet • Doll
Acrylic medium • Wood • Wood glue

1. The cigar brand, *La Palina*, intrigued me. Was the young lady on the box—perhaps an actress or singer—La Palina? With a few clicks of a computer mouse, I found that Palina is a town in Italy. Additional clicks led me to images from the title page of Fabritio Caroso's sixteenth-century dance manual *Il Ballarino*. Here I found a reference to *Palina Rustica*. I printed out the pages for reference. Then I searched through my store of images and found the exercising girls (an illustration from a nineteenth-century book on healthful living) and the postcard of the dancing couple in rustic costume. Then I put the project aside for a couple of weeks.

2. I had the small plastic dancing girls on hand and covered them with gold leaf. At some point, I came across the doll in an antique store and knew I had to use it in this box. Unfortunately, the box wouldn't close with the doll inside. Once again, I put the project aside.

3. After seeing a show of daguerreotypes in a museum, I was intrigued with the ghostly appearance of the images. I photocopied the doll and my other imagery onto water slide transfer paper (see page 18).

4. I painted the interior of the box white, leaving the printed label intact. Then I added background layers of printed tissue and other papers to the interior of the box with acrylic medium.

5. I coated the box's paper-covered surfaces with a thin coat of acrylic varnish to prepare them for applying the water slide transfers.

6. I cut a piece of clear acrylic to fit inside the box. I cut out and painted two narrow strips of thin basswood to support the acrylic above the bottom of the box. Then I glued the two pieces to the inside of the box.

7. I cut out and applied the water slide transfer images to the clear acrylic and the box, glued the gilded dancing girls to the box, and placed the image of the doll on the basswood supports.

8. I store the postcard inside the box.

Dolly's Diary

"I recently came across some old photographs of my grandparents that I had never seen before. Instead of seeing my grandmother, Dolly, I saw a person I didn't know: one full of life, confidence, and passion. One photograph really caught my attention. It was a picture of my grandparents sitting on a park bench. I couldn't get over how mesmerized Edwin seemed to be with Dolly and how confident Dolly seemed in that knowledge. It was this photo that inspired me to create Dolly's Diary."

Chris Young, DESIGNER

MATERIALS   Metal CD tin • Sandpaper • Gesso • Decorative papers • Walnut ink
Small spatula • Acrylic modeling paste • Inks • Rubber stamp • Copper metal sheet
Liver of sulphur (or other oxidizing material) • Brads • Industrial strength glue • Acrylic medium
Silk ribbon • Thin chipboard or heavy card stock • Charms and embellishments

1. Chris lightly sanded the tin and gave the surfaces a coat of gesso.

2. She glued decorative paper to the front of the tin with acrylic medium, then lightly sanded it to distress it. She adhered her imagery to the paper with medium. Then she stained the paper and images with a commercially made walnut ink.

3. Chris spread a thin coat of acrylic modeling paste to portions of the surface and pressed a rubber stamp directly into the wet paste. When the paste dried completely, she sponged inks on to color the paste.

Designer Tips

Use acrylic modeling paste to add texture and dimension to your work. You can rubber-stamp directly into wet paste, just be sure you clean your stamp immediately after stamping!

• Press sponges, hardware cloth, lace, or any textured material into the wet paste to create texture.
• Lay a stencil on your surface, spread the paste on the stencil, and carefully lift up the stencil to reveal a dimensional shape on the surface.
• Spread a layer of paste and embed small dimensional articles (buttons, charms, and the like).
• Build up thicker layers a little at a time and then carve designs into the dried paste.

4. From a sheet of copper, Chris cut two decorative strips and a small frame shape. She made small holes in the metal and oxidized the copper with a patina solution (see page 81).

5. She stained additional text—a photocopy of a dictionary entry for "dolly"—with walnut ink and glued it to the frame.

6. Chris placed the metal pieces on the lid and the marked the locations of the holes. She made holes in the lid, then glued the metal strips and frame to the lid, and used brads to mimic rivets. A piece of decorative paper, cut to fit the inside of the lid, covers the legs of the brads.

7. Chris created pages on thin chipboard cut to fit inside the tin. She collaged decorative papers, imagery, and text to both sides of each page.

Daguerreotype of
A Young Girl Reading

"Years before I made this project I'd looked at real daugerreotypes in antique stores. Often these boxes contain velvet and metal, two materials I love. The idea to create a daugerreotype evolved in my head years before I actually created one. The miniature cigar boxes I found inspired me to create this project."

Katherine Sullivan, DESIGNER

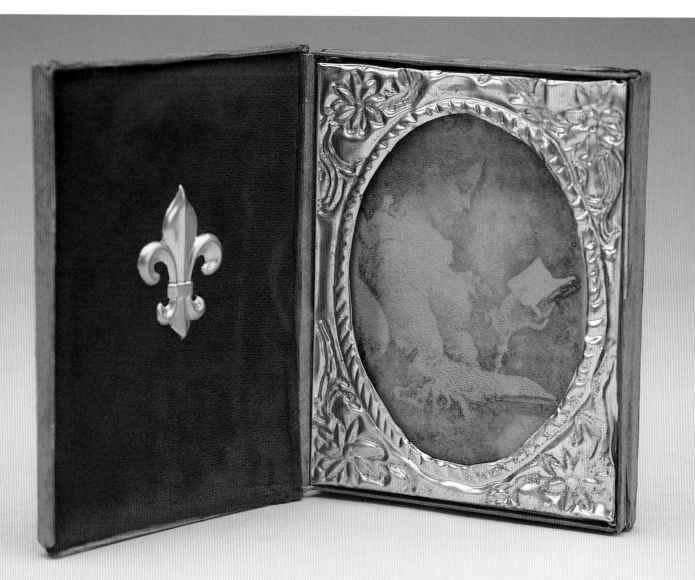

MATERIALS   Paperboard cigar miniatures box • Stamping inks • Rubber stamps • Mat board • Foam-core board • Velvet • Thin batting • Acrylic medium • Tissue paper • Metal charm • Embossing metal • Fiber mailing envelope

1. Katherine worked with a small cardboard box that she found in a tobacco shop.

2. At a glass shop, she had one piece of glass cut slightly smaller than the interior measurements of the box.

3. She cleaned the glass to remove any fingerprints. Katherine chose a rubber stamp image of *Young Girl Reading* by Jean-Honoré Fragonard (1732-1806) to stamp on the glass. She cut a piece of foam-core board to size to support the glass.

Designer Tip

You can add an image to glass in one of the following ways if you can't find a stamp image you wish to use.

• Photocopy a vintage family photo and adhere it face down on the glass with a clear-drying acrylic medium.

• Copy an image onto water slide transfer paper (page 18) and apply it to the glass.

• Create a packing tape transfer (page 20) and apply it face down on the glass with medium.

4. Katherine cut a piece of mat board to fit inside the lid of the box, then cut a layer of thin batting and tacked it to the board with glue. She cut a piece of velvet somewhat larger than the mat board, placed it on the batting, and glued the edges to the back of the board. Finally, she glued a brass charm to the velvet.

5. Katherine brushed a thin coat of acrylic medium on the box's outer surfaces. She crumpled tissue paper and placed it on the surface, but didn't attempt to smooth the wrinkles and creases in the tissue. She used additional medium on a brush to press the tissue to the surface. When the tissue dried, Katherine applied layers of stamping ink to the tissue to achieve the look of aged leather. She then gave the tissue a coat of acrylic varnish tinted with a bit of acrylic paint.

6. Katherine created an embossed metal frame to surround the stamped image.

How to Emboss a Metal Frame

Practice embossing on a scrap of soft metal before working on your frame. Experimenting allows you to learn just how hard to press. Or, use embossing techniques you may already know.

• Cut out a soft metal sheet one inch (2.54 cm) wider and longer than the glass.

• Draw an oval on the metal. You'll cut it out later to frame the image on the glass.

• Use brass embossing stencils as guides for designs, or sketch your own designs lightly on the metal.

• Place the metal on a magazine or mouse pad. Use an embossing tool (or an empty ball-point pen) to trace your designs.

• Turn the metal over. Trace around the outside edges of your embossed designs to give them further definition.

• Cut out the marked oval with a craft knife.

7. Katherine sandwiched the glass image between the embossed metal frame and foam core board. She wrapped the metal edges around the glass and foam core. Then she glued the metal to the board.

8. Katherine's box wasn't hinged. She created a hinge with a length of material cut from a mailing envelope. She glued the material to the bottom of the box and up the side, then down the side of the lid and onto the lid. She smoothed the hinge and aligned the edges of the top and bottom of the box side by side. Then she held the aligned edges together with bulldog clips until the material dried. She used stamping inks to color the hinge.

9. She used a small amount of glue to hold the framed image and the velvet covered board in the box.

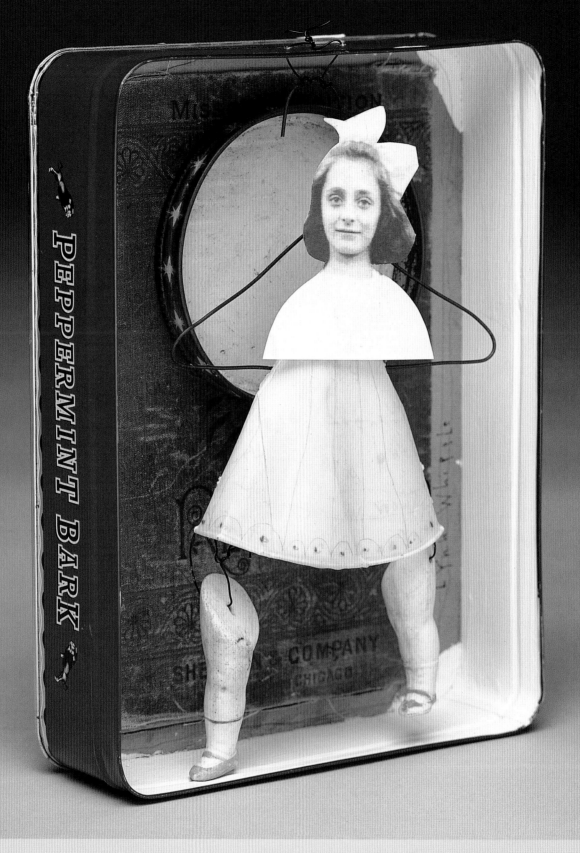

Peppermint Girl

"I love old photos. I love the stories they tell and the stories I get to tell for them. Old photos give me insight and allow me to peek into others' lives. I'm keenly aware that we're all flawed, and looking at old photos helps me embrace this knowledge. Hidden flaws and shortcomings frequently make a person more endearing. Photos are a great tool in helping me explore the human story through my artwork. Plus, I love a good laugh; they crack me up!"

Lynn Whipple, DESIGNER

MATERIALS Tin box • Color photocopy of old photo • Foam core board • Cone-shape paper cup Pastels • Beeswax • Jar lid • China doll legs • Decorative papers • Steel wire

1. Lynn made a color copy of an old photograph and glued it to a piece of foam core board. She cut out the head and shoulders of the photograph.

2. She added a bit of subtle color to the paper cup "dress" with pencil and pastel. Then, she gave the cup a coat of beeswax.

Designer Tip

Add sheen and patina to almost any surface with a coat of beeswax. Melt the beeswax in a heat-proof container over low heat until it is liquid. Quickly dip the object in the wax and lift it out. Let the wax drip back into the container. You can also use a brush to paint the melted wax. Build up thicker layers of wax a little at a time.

3. She attached the china doll legs to the hem of the dress with thin steel wire.

4. To create a clothes hanger out of heavy wire, Lynn sketched out the shape of the hanger on paper, and used the sketch as a template to bend the wire. She began at the hook and worked to the bottom of the hanger. She threaded the straight wire through the top of the dress at about shoulder height. Finally, she bent the wire to finish the hanger shape.

5. Lynn glued the girl's head to the dress and hanger.

6. She painted the interior of the box, collaged the surface with paper, and glued an old book cover to the surface.

7. In the top of the box, Lynn punched a small hole with an awl. She attached wire to the hanger and threaded the wire through the hole to suspend the doll.

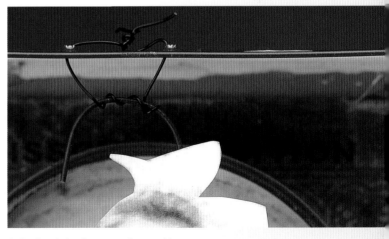

A simple solution for suspending an object

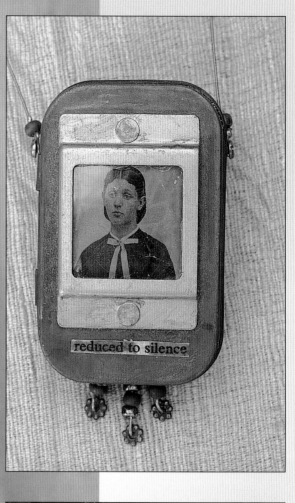

reduced to silence

Sign your work.

Assemblage Jewelry: Hidden Within

"I love to create curiosity! These small tin containers make people want to know what's inside. Once you grab their attention and pique their curiosity, you've opened the way for great conversation. There's nothing more powerful than using an actual piece of history. Why would I risk altering a piece of history? Well, there are thousands of these little pieces of history out there. The moment I change them into a wearable piece of art they take on a new life. As an artist, I think it's a great way to get people to talk about your art."

Jane Wynn, DESIGNER

MATERIALS Small tins • Cable wire • Jewelry glue or epoxy • Miniature flathead screws and nuts • Patina solution • Acrylic paint • Text • Tintypes Small metal frame • Eyelets • Assorted beads • Crimp beads • Necklace clasp

1. Jane removed the painted surface of the small tin boxes with a nontoxic paint stripper. She used a patina solution purchased in a craft store to oxidize the metal.

2. She marked the position for the small brass frame on the box. Then she used a drill bit the same size as the eyelets (see page 82) to create holes. Jane used the tiniest drill bit she owned to make holes on the sides and bottom edge of the box.

3. In the frame, she placed the tintype and text she selected and secured them with a small amount of glue.

4. She riveted the frame to the box with eyelets (see page 82).

5. Using a combination of wire and jump rings, Jane decorated the tin with beads and found metal objects. She lightly applied gold acrylic paint to the tin to complement the brass frame.

6. Jane used thin cable wire to create a necklace.

How to Make the Necklace

- Cut two pieces of cable wire to the length you desire.
- Place two nuts on each screw. You'll need one screw for each side of the box. Tighten the first nut up against the screw head. Run the second nut close to, but not touching, the first.
- Make a small loop of wire around the screw shaft, between the two nuts. Hold the loop in place with a crimp bead. Tighten the second nut to catch the loop securely. Repeat the process with the second wire.
- Slip a screw in one of the holes you drilled for the necklace. Use one or two nuts to hold the screw in place. Use flat jewelry pliers to turn the nut if you can't do it with your fingers. Attach the second screw on the opposite side.
- Thread beads or charms on the wires as desired.
- Slip a crimp bead on the end of a wire. Thread on the clasp and form a loop. Slip the end of the wire back through the crimp bead, adjust the loop, and crimp the bead.

Designer Tip

It's easy to set eyelets when you have clear access to the front and back of the piece you're working on. It can be tricky (if not downright impossible) to set eyelets when you can't get your hammer or setting tool into position. I finesse my way around the problem by using a brad instead of an eyelet. Simply insert the brad through the holes and spread the legs on the opposite side.

Gallery

I was fascinated with the concept that humans need to be constrained by rules of law, imposed rather than innate. The men in this piece look as if they would like to sue each other.

PATRICIA CHAPMAN, *Rule of the Law*, 2003
Printed graphics, wood, twine, briefcase, rulers, wood box, 25½ x 32¼ x 4 in.
(64.8 x 82 x 10.2 cm)
Collection of Jane and Al Schwartz
Photo by artist

PATRICIA CHAPMAN, *Pearls of Wisdom*, 2003
Chalkware bust, metal faucet, glass box, wallpaper brush, metal frame, polymer clay, 20¾ x 16¾ x 4½ in.
(52.7 x 42.5 x 11.4 cm)
Photo by artist

I was inspired by the vacuous look on the face of the bust in this piece. He looked as if every bit of thought and wisdom had been drained from his head.

PATRICIA CHAPMAN, *A Good Cup of Coffee*, 2003
Vintage coffee can, figurine, metal frame, printed graphic, wood box, 20 x 9 x 4½ in. (50.8 x 22.9 x 11.4 cm)
Collection of Bunny Tobias and Charles Greeley
Photo by artist

With this piece I focused on the idea of prayer as the essence of hope and how hopes can be large or small, obtainable or not.

NICOLE TUGGLE, *Shelter*, 2003
Metal mailbox, photo, thorns, feathers, paper, dictionary definition, beeswax, rusted metal, 8½ x 13 x 3½ in. (21.6 x 33 x 8.9 cm)
Photos by Steve Mann

MARY J. TAFOYA
Sojourner Truth, 2002
Hinged candy tin, photo-edited imagery, photo corners, handmade accordion book, acrylic paint, 3¾ x 2½ x ¾ in. (9.5 x 6.4 x 1.9 cm)
Photos by Pat Berrett

I often create tin box shrines to women who stir my soul. This altered tin is a tribute to suffragette Sojourner Truth, whose historic "Ain't I A Woman" speech is contained in the pages of the pop-out accordion book inside.

JOSEPH BORZOTTA, *Smokin'*, 1995
Drawing and mixed media, 8 x 8 x 8 in. (20.3 x 20.3 x 20.3 cm)
Photo by artist

CAROLE AUSTIN *Day of the Dead*, 2002
Cigar box, mixed materials
Photos by artist

Urban Remnants, 2003
Cigar box, wood, paper, paint; collage,
8¾ x 7¼ x 2½ in. (22.2 x 18.4 x 6.4 cm)
Photos by artist

*I have always placed cigar boxes in the same category as the circus, as it helps
define the allure. The cigar box, like the circus, has just a little bit of the forbidden
in it. After all, as children, smoking was not allowed and to do it was risky business
(as was running away with the circus). Oh, the stories of circus life and sideshows
that left us wide eyed. Both the circus and cigar boxes are brightly colored, downright
gaudy, and humble, something quite enchanting to a child. The boxes had wonderful
names like Roi-Tan and Panatela, which we couldn't even pronounce. But we'd
make up our own stories about their origins from exotic places; the enchantment
seemed to carry over right into adulthood for many of us.*

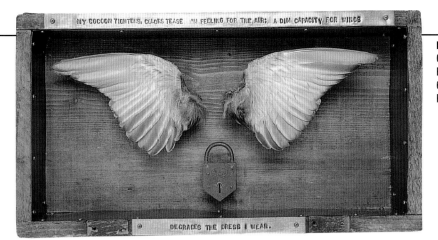

RON SAWYER, *My Cocoon Tightens*, 1999
Old wood box, bird wings, rusty lock,
Emily Dickinson poem; stamped on copper,
6⅜ x 12 x 3¼ in. (16.2 x 30.5 x 8.2 cm)
Photo by artist

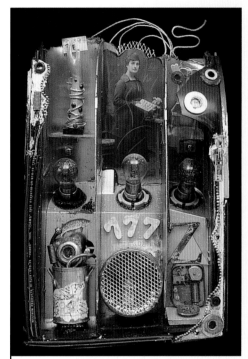

DEBORAH HAYNER
Cyber Etiquette, 1999
Mixed media, 12 x 7¾ x 3¾ in. (30.5 x 19.7 x 9.5 cm)

RON SAWYER, *The Sea*, 2001
Old wood instrument shipping box,
sea shell, vintage photo, poem by artist,
9¾ x 8¾ x 2½ in. (24.7 x 22.2 x 6.4 cm)
Photo by artist

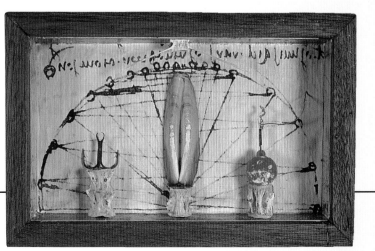

SHARI KADISON, *Exhibition*, 2000
Paper, bone, shell, fishhook, styrofoam; box construction,
5 x 7 x 1½ in. (12.7 x 17.8 x 3.8 cm)
Photo by Chris Green

Basics

BOBBY HANSSON
Envelope, 2004

A flat surface is an almost perfect surface for altered art. It's easy to embellish, imagery is easily applied, and it doesn't require difficult adaptations of special techniques.

Many artists create small flat works to flex their creative muscles for larger pieces. Or they may make tiny works of fine art like Donald Evans's altered postcards (page 12). Some artists specifically create small cards, charms, or tags to exchange with other artists (page 103) or to use as embellishments in other altered art pieces (see page 110). Artists participating in mail art exchanges create unique postcards or casually sketch on one-of-a-kind envelopes.

Postcards, playing cards, puzzles, and game boards are all fair game for creating altered art. You can purchase new or used items to work on. The variety of imagery on postcards provide a perfect canvas for collage. Game boards, with their arcane markings and symbols, offer intriguing possibilities for altered art. Create an entire deck of altered playing cards for yourself or to exchange with others. Loteria cards (used in a Mexican form of bingo), children's game cards, and tarot cards offer a wealth of imagery to work on.

WORKING ON FLAT SURFACES

It's easy to simply glue items to flat surfaces and there's nothing wrong with doing so. The items you adhere to flat surfaces won't roll off as you glue them (unless, of course, you're working on the surfaces upright!) and you don't have to worry about gluing things to uneven surfaces. But don't limit yourself to simply gluing items. Use staples and brads, tape, or even stitch items to your flat surfaces with wire or thread.

Eyelets, Eyelets, and Grommets!

You see eyelets (and grommets) everywhere and applied to everything these days. Not only are they in fashion, it's simple to set eyelets or grommets on thin, flat surfaces. The technique for setting both of them in place is remarkably similar. However, grommets are larger and set using two pieces—unlike an eyelet's single-piece construction. Follow the manufacturer's instructions when setting a grommet.

• Punch holes in your object with a hole punch or drive punch. Make sure the holes you create are the same diameter as the stem of your eyelet. Place an eyelet in the punched hole and turn the object over onto a hard surface.

• Flare the stem of the eyelet using a hammer and setting tool.

❋ Designer Tip

Don't rule out using eyelets on thicker materials if you really like the look. Drill a hole into or through the material. Set the eyelet in place with a dab of industrial strength glue on the stem.

Playing Cards

"I started drawing on playing cards that I found on the street when I lived in Brooklyn. I remember drawing a traditional quilt pattern that I was working with at the time on the first one I found. The pattern fit perfectly in the negative space of a six of diamonds. At the time, they were just sketches, but later they became more deliberate. Playing cards provide a surface that already has a pattern, a history, and connotations of gambling and chance for creating narratives about specific incidences in my life. I work intuitively and spontaneously. Pieces evolve as I go, without a preconceived idea of what they will become. The small format of a playing card forces me to concentrate on one moment."

Jen Swearington, DESIGNER

MATERIALS   **Playing cards • Collage materials • Acrylic medium • Gesso • Inks Acrylic paint • Thread • Typed text**

1. Jen adhered various collage materials—patterned paper and images—to the cards with acrylic medium. She cut windows or holes in opaque materials to expose the symbols or numbers on the cards before she applied the opaque materials.

2. On some cards, Jen applied layers of gesso or paint. Then she scratched into the paint to reveal the layer underneath.

3. Jen typed text directly onto the cards with an old typewriter. She stitched the cards by machine, but she hand-stitched dimensional elements onto the cards.

4. With acrylic medium she adhered scraps of paper dress pattern to the tin. Jen pierced around the metal lid with a small drill bit to allow items to be stitched to the tin. Finally, she lined the tin with fabric attached with double-stick tape.

More Playing Card Ideas

"I wanted to create some unique cards to trade with other artists or to attach to blank greeting cards. Here are some of the techniques I used to create them."

Terry Taylor, DESIGNER

1. Adhere thin oriental papers or tissue paper to both sides of a card with acrylic medium. Covering both sides will prevent warping.

2. Add borders to cards with decorative papers or rubber-stamped patterns around the outer edge.

3. Stitch on simple decorative elements such as charms. Add specialty eyelets or eyelet letters. Strengthen punched holes with eyelets, and thread on decorative fibers.

4. Rubber-stamp or collage text onto cards.

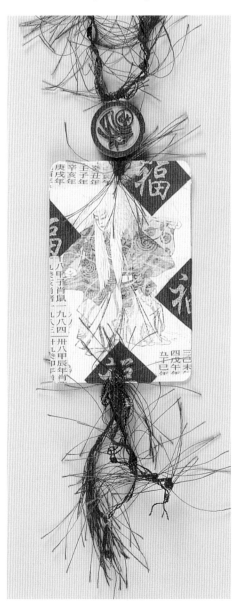

Artist Trading Cards

Artist trading cards (ATCs) are miniature works of art. They're just about the same size as your brother's old baseball cards or a playing card, measuring 2½ x 3½ inches (6.4 cm x 8.9 cm).

Artists create ATCs either as one-of-a-kind originals or in small printed or photocopied editions. Each card is signed and, if part of an edition, numbered. In general they're created on heavy cardstock. No money changes hands—cards are traded one-for-one. Some artists create ATCs and use them as business cards or like the calling cards of the nineteenth century (page 115).

The original concept provided a face-to-face forum for artists to trade small works of art and, in turn, ideas with each other. Our digital age has spawned on-line exchanges. In on-line exchanges, a call for participants usually includes a proposed theme for the ATC swap. Participants create a set number of cards, which are sent to individual participants or to a single person who distributes sets of cards to all of the participants.

Artists who meet together in groups or participate in workshops have expanded the concept of the ATC to include handmade charms, unique business cards, and other altered objects. All's fair for trading!

TRACY ROOS
ATCs, 2004

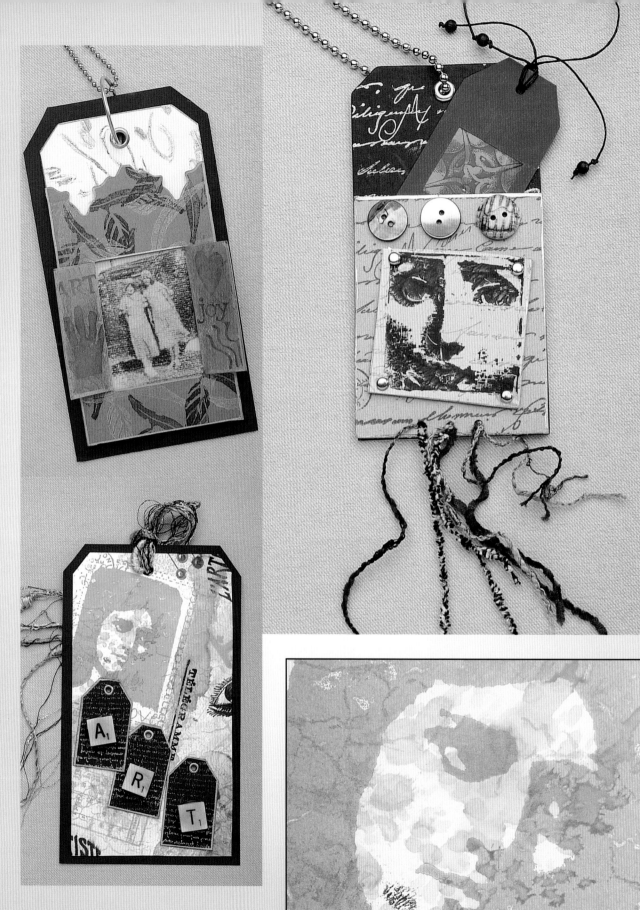

Creative Tags

"Tags are an open ticket to anywhere. Those who know me know my favorite phrase is 'There are no rules.' For me, tags are a canvas for creativity. I can attach one to a card or add several to a page in an altered book, creating both dimension and intrigue. Tags are a way to make a statement...they allow each and every one of us to explore our individual creativity."

Jane Powell, DESIGNER

MATERIALS   Mat board • Acetate • Eyelets

1. Tags don't have to be created on purchased, paper shapes. Jane used both a commercial die cut machine and a craft knife to cut shapes from mat board. She cut copper and corrugated metal tag shapes by hand with metal shears.

2. Jane created imagery with rubber stamps and photo transfer techniques on both paper and acetate, and mounted paper images under mica.

3. She added text to the tags with rubber stamps.

4. Jane used eyelets to attach frames, pockets, and some embellishments. She drilled holes on the metal tags and used hole punches to create holes in the mat board tags. She wired or glued embellishments to the tags.

5. The tags may be worn or hung for display. Jane threaded fibers or chains through the tops of the tags. To strengthen the punched holes on the paper tags she added eyelets; metal tags need no reinforcement.

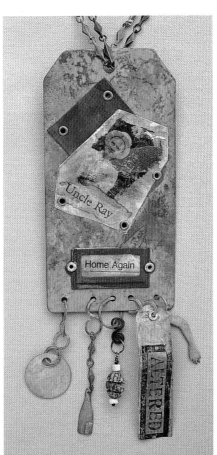

Metal slide frame with stamp image on transparency (top)
Verdigris patina solution applied to copper (left)
Brads glued into drilled holes in clear acrylic (above)

Altered Puzzle

"This vintage puzzle was a true mystery. I didn't know what the image was until I'd assembled it! It turned out to be a view of Venice, which reminded me of the delightful little movie A Little Romance. *The film tells the story of two young teens' blossoming first love, the concern of their disapproving parents, and their decision to run away to Venice. In Venice, a charming pickpocket tells them if they kiss in a gondola under the Bridge of Sighs, as the bells of the Campanile ring at sunset, their love will last forever. Visitors to my artist's open studio event were asked to share their own 'little romances' by writing down how they met their true love—and how they knew it was indeed true love—on the back of the assembled and embellished puzzle."*

Luann Udell, DESIGNER

MATERIALS   Jigsaw puzzle • Assorted decorative papers • Art tissue paper • Acrylic medium
Permanent ink markers • Acrylic paints • Rubber stamps • Ink pads • Postage stamps
Paper packing tape

1. Once Luann assembled the puzzle, she carefully turned it over.

Designer Tips

Vintage puzzles often don't have a picture of the completed puzzle on the box. When using second-hand puzzles, make sure it's complete, unless the idea of missing pieces appeals to you. Avoid purchasing puzzles that are mildewed or smell musty.

Assemble your puzzle on a sheet of foam-core or poster board. When all the pieces are in place, cover the puzzle with a second sheet and carefully turn the puzzle over. It's always handy—but not absolutely necessary—to have an extra set of helping hands for this process.

2. She brushed the back of the puzzle with a light coat of acrylic medium, then placed a sheet of tissue paper on the wet medium and smoothed it into place.

3. Luann selected materials relating to the theme—Italian postage stamps, rubber stamp images, assorted papers, and faux postage stamps—and collaged them onto the back of the puzzle. Some elements were collaged on the puzzle image as well.

How to Make Faux Postage Stamps

- Stamp an image on paper or on paper packing tape. Add additional color to the image, if desired.
- Lightly sketch a stamp shape around the image. Stamps can be rectangular, square, or even triangular.
- Use decorative-edge scissors to cut out the shape. Use glue or moisten the backing of the packing tape to adhere your faux stamp.

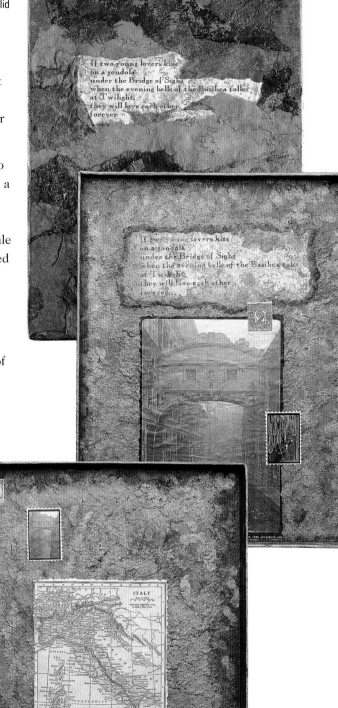

4. Luann added text to the puzzle with permanent markers, rubber stamps, and printed materials. Then she allowed visitors to her studio to add their own text.

5. She held the completed puzzle up to the light to help locate the lines of individual pieces. She used a pin to prick guidelines around blocks of text, then cut along the lines with a sharp craft knife. Then she drew along the borders of each piece with a pale marker to give the individual pieces a more finished look. Each piece was given a finish coat of acrylic varnish.

6. The original box the puzzle came in was not in good shape. Luann adhered a variety of decorative and handmade papers to a new box. Many layers of torn paper were adhered to the box, covering it entirely. She added both text and imagery to the box surface.

Designer Tip

Using a small paintbrush, draw a line with water on the paper you wish to tear. Gently but firmly tear along this wet line. Using this technique will give your paper a beautiful, deckle edge.

7. Luann sponged gold and bronze accents on the surface of the box. She traced fine lines around some of the paper shapes that resembled puzzle pieces, hinting at the contents of the box. She brushed a final coat of acrylic varnish on the box's surfaces.

Original collages

Slides and Fobs

"I wanted to create small editions with collages to exchange with other artists, but I didn't want to simply make a flat card. I chose to use fobs and slide mounts as frames for the collages, which made these small editions even more special. Create your own for exchanging or for embellishing your altered art projects."

Terry Taylor, DESIGNER

MATERIALS   Recycled slide mounts • Color transparencies • Color photocopies • Decorative papers • Plastic key chain fobs • Wire • Beads • Eyelets • Metal charms • Jump rings

I scanned my collaged images and sized them to fit inside the slide mounts and fobs. Then, I printed the scans on both paper and transparencies.

Slide Mounts

1. Our freelance photographers here at Lark provide us with a endless supply of slide mounts, so I recycled some of them for this project. I carefully prised them open with the tip of a dull table knife to remove the film. Then I covered the mounts with decorative paper.

How to Cover a Slide Mount

• Prise open a slide mount.
• Coat one side of the slide mount with acrylic medium.
• Lay the mount on paper and cover it with a sheet of waxed paper. Weight the mount with a heavy object. Allow the adhered paper to dry, preferably overnight.
• Trim the openings and around the edges of the slide mount with a sharp craft knife. Leave the paper between the hinged part of the mount intact.

2. I punched a hole in one corner of the mount, marked the position of the hole on the opposite side, and punched a second hole.

3. I chose an image on paper or film, trimmed it to fit, and glued it to the inside of the mount. I placed a small amount of glue on the inside of the mount before I snapped the mount shut.

4. I set eyelets in the punched holes.

Fobs

1. I mounted photocopied images on card stock and trimmed them to fit inside the fob.

2. I drilled tiny holes into the bottom edge of a few fobs. I threaded a short length of wire through each hole, twisted one short end onto the wire, then threaded the beads in place. The end of each wire was coiled to hold the beads in place.

Scanned collages printed on paper and transparency

3. I created additional fobs containing original text and imagery mounted on card stock. I glued or riveted brass charms to the fobs and attached chains on these fobs to create necklaces.

Altered Parchessi Board

"The HOME plate on the Parcheesi board is so graphically compelling it dictated the choice of home as the theme for this piece. I tried to stay within a specific time frame—1940 to 1950—when choosing my images and embellishments. I used the board's bright color scheme when I chose the elements to be used in this piece."

Jean Tomaso Moore, DESIGNER

MATERIALS • Game board • Tracing paper • Acrylic paint • Miniature wooden architectural ornaments • Eyelets • Eyelet letters • Rubber stamps • Ink pad • Wire • Beads and charms • Acrylic medium • White glue • Industrial strength adhesive • Ribbon • Wood

1. Jean gave the board a thin coat of acrylic medium and allowed it to dry. Then she brushed the board with a thin wash of brown acrylic paint, which she immediately wiped off. Jean treated all of the paper elements and imagery she wished to apply to the board using the same process.

2. She traced the various geometric shapes on the board onto tracing paper to create templates. These templates provided guides for cutting out the paper images. Then she adhered the images to the geometric shapes with gel medium.

3. Jean drilled holes matching the diameter of the eyelet stems into the board. She glued eyelets into

Text applied with packing tape transfer (page 20)

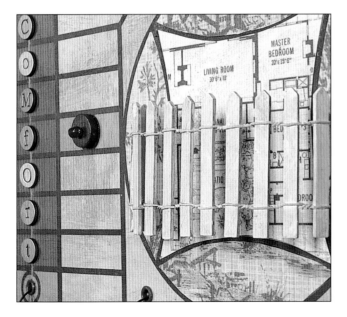

the holes with industrial strength adhesive. The metal eyelet letters that spell comfort, refuge, and safety were attached in the same manner.

4. She adhered the wooden architectural elements to the board with industrial strength adhesive, and used a length of ribbon glued to the edges of the board to create a more finished appearance.

5. Jean drilled tiny holes into some of the decorative elements hanging from the board. She threaded them onto wire and attached the wire to the board.

6. For supports that let the board stand away from the wall and allow the wired elements to hang freely, Jean cut two lengths of wood to fit the back of the board and attached them with industrial strength adhesive.

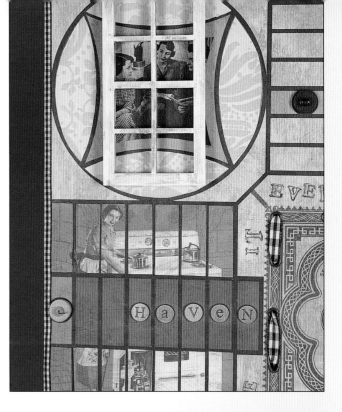

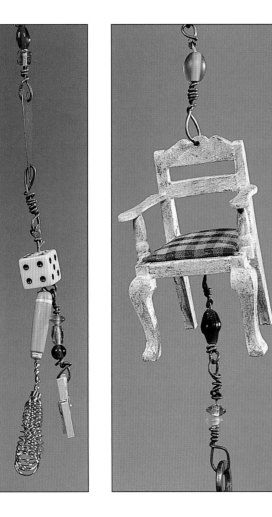

Calling Cards

Calling cards date back to the Victorian age, when well-to-do families conformed to rigid social rules. Face-to-face interaction took place only after several cards passed back and forth, and elaborate rules soon arose, dictating how to choose the proper cards and when, where, and how to use them. A caller could indicate the nature of the visit by folding down one of the corners. Men could leave their wives' cards, but women couldn't leave their husbands' cards until midcentury.

Each lady of the house had regular at-home days for receiving visitors. The time of day for the visit depended on the relationship between the visitor and the hostess and on the nature of the visit. Ceremonial calls involving marriage, childbirth, and condolences or congratulations took place between three and four o'clock. Semi-ceremonial visits took place between four and five, and intimate calls between five and six. Sunday was for family and close friends only.

Custom required that a visitor simply leave a card without asking whether the mistress was home. The mistress would decide how to respond. If the visitor was told the mistress was not at home, it was seen as a clear rejection. If the mistress sent a card to the caller informally, that meant she did not wish to further their relationship. Those lucky enough to receive a formal response to a formal card had hope the relationship could go forward.

Although cards would develop into ornate affairs later in the nineteenth century, proper families stuck with a stark, simple style. According to *The Habits of Good Society: A Handbook of Etiquette for Ladies and Gentlemen* (1859), cards should be printed in simple Italian script, not Gothic or Roman letters, and without any flourishes. A card's style indicated one's station in life, and high-society cards often displayed only the name of the individual, addresses being added later on.

Cards printed with vibrant, colorful images or trimmed with elegant, silky fringes and feathers are popular collectibles today. Some cards made with heavier stock were designed with hidden signatures. Each one would have a die-cut illustration, called a scrap, which could be lifted to reveal the caller's name. Calligraphers—called penmen at the time—were paid the equivalent of 10 cents to draft a dozen cards, often with birds, banners, and other embellishments.

Today, artists have revived this once popular social custom—minus the byzantine rules—by exchanging hand-crafted artist trading cards. Even the virtual world of the Internet has reinvented the custom. Web designers who visit other sites often leave electronic cards in the site's guest book.

Altered Postcards

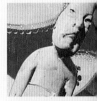

"A large collection of postcards provides me with a constant source of inspiration, imagery, and working surfaces. Mine are stored by type (really and truly!) in storage boxes. I purchase cards whenever and wherever I find them: in airports, antique shops, motels, and museums. I also coerce friends and coworkers who are traveling to bring back cards. I send the altered cards to mail art exchanges (page 119), use them for casual correspondence, or send them as special greeting cards to friends."

Terry Taylor, DESIGNER

MATERIALS   Postcards • Glue • Collage elements

1. Cards with identical images or that are similar in appearance (frequently these are sets) are fun to work with. Cut a card into strips and glue it on top of another. If you have identical cards, cut out elements from one and add them to the other.

2. Punch out shapes with large, decorative punches on two or more similar cards. Replace the punched shapes with shapes from different cards. Glue a small piece of paper to the back of the card to hold the shape in place.

3. Weave two identical or similar cards together. Cut evenly spaced slits in one using a sharp craft knife. Cut the second card into similarly sized strips. Weave the strips over and under the cut slits.

4. Cut out unrelated images and adhere them to a card to create a disquieting or amusing new image.

Designer Tip
I don't photocopy vintage cards to work on, unless I'm truly attached to the unaltered image. I prefer working on actual cards. I keep the original work, and mail photocopied editions that are mounted on mat board or card stock.

5. Use your altered cards to create new pieces. Photocopy the cards and transfer the image (using

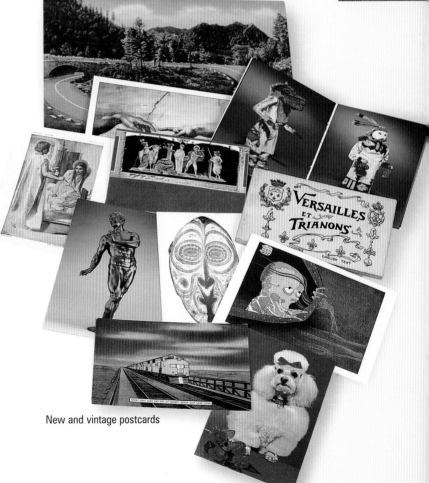

New and vintage postcards

the transfer method of your choice) to wood or foam-core board. Lightly sand or paint directly on the image; add dimensional elements, if desired.

Designer Tip

Mail your altered postcards, but keep in mind that our mailing system is automated. Dimensional embellishments may prevent a card's safe passage through the system (page 119). If you're adding dimensional elements, send the postcard in a padded envelope or small box.

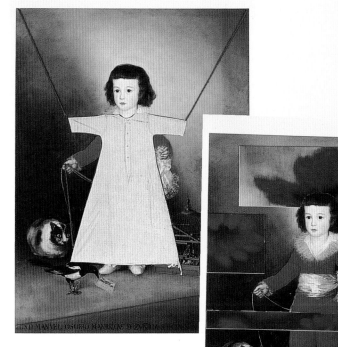

Variations on Goya's portrait of *Don Manuel Osorio Manrique De Zuñiga*

Collage on
William Matthew Prior's
Child in a Red Dress

Postcard collage and image transfer on wood

Mail Art

Mail art was popularized by artists such as Ray Johnson and his New York Correspondence School in the 1950s and 1960s, but the roots of the movement go back much earlier to the postal experiments of the Dadaists and Futurists. Some of the first examples were created by Marcel Duchamp. He sent four postcards in 1916 to his next-door neighbor. The text of the postcards was linguistically perfect, but had absolutely no meaning (a Dadaist twist).

Johnson studied at the innovative Black Mountain College in the late 1940s. At Black Mountain he was no doubt introduced to and influenced by the works of artists who participated in the unofficial Dada movement in the early part of the twentieth century. He began to give his work away through the mail, asking others to collaborate with him in creating layered mail-art collages by adding to his work and returning it to him. In addition to Johnson's New York Correspondence School, the Image Bank in Canada, as well as networks in Japan, Germany, and Eastern Europe began circulating art through the mail. By the early 1970s, the Whitney Museum exhibited works by the Correspondence School, and mail art has now expanded into correspondence dinners, congresses, and the zine network.

Artists Daniel Farrell and Richard Kegler tested the abilities of New York postal employees between 1990 and 1996 by sending more than 200 mail-art pieces between Buffalo and Albany. One such work was a 4 x 5-inch (10.2 x 12.7 cm) sheet of glass sandwiched between a copper screen and a piece of Mylar, sent with the expectation that it would end up shattered. The post office prevailed and delivered the piece intact. Farrell and Kegler stopped sending their art through the mail after postal regulations, favoring speed and efficiency, resulted in the return of most of their pieces.

The United States Postal Service requires that you print or type the delivery address parallel to the longest side of a package, envelope, or card. To qualify for postcard rates, a card must be between 3¼ and 4¼ inches (8.3 and 10.8 cm) in height, 5 and 6 inches (12.7 and 15.2 cm) in width. Mailing unusual sizes, shapes, or weights may require additional postage or may be undeliverable. The post office prefers addresses printed in black or blue ink, which can be sorted automatically. Other colors, such as red or silver, are acceptable, but have to be hand-sorted and take longer to reach the destination.

TERRY TAYLOR
Symptoms of the Trance, 1983
Altered postcard, 3½ x 5½ in.
(8.9 x 14 cm)
Collection of Ron Meisner
Photo by Evan Bracken

Gallery

G. MCLARTY
Clockwise from left:

Postcard, 2002
Copper, enamel, collage, mica, 24-karat gold leaf,
stamp, 5½ x 3½ x ¼ in. (14 x 8.9 x .6 cm)
Photo by Jack Zilker

Postcard, 2002
Copper, enamel, collage, mica, stamp, thread,
5½ x 3½ x ¼ in. (14 x 8.9 x .6 cm)
Photo by Jack Zilker

Postcard, 2002
Copper, enamel, collage, mica, stamp,
5½ x 3½ x ¼ in. (14 x 8.9 x .6 cm)
Photo by Jack Zilker

LISA GLICKSMAN, *WWW.Laundry*, 2003
Salvaged book pages, buttons, found objects,
laundry lint, miniature clothespins,
9 x 37 in. (22.9 x 94 cm)
Photos by Uri Korn

DAWN SOUTHWORTH, *Holiday*, 1995
Mixed media, wood, fabric, paper, antique
journal entry, found painting, 23 x 46 x 4 in.
(58.4 x 117 x 10.2 cm)
Photo by Dana Salvo

*The burns, scars, sutures, and gestural marks function not only
as authorial traces but connote issues of genetics, biology, cellular
growth, or, conversely, blisters and wounds. Shifting surfaces,
eroded and renewed, become embodiments of disease and death
with affirmations of healing and regeneration.*

CLAUDINE HELLMUTH

Little Friend, 2003
Acrylic paint, dress pattern tissue, romance novel
text, crossword puzzle, ink drawing,
5 x 7 in. (12.7 x 17.8 cm)

The Epitome of Grace and Style, 2003
Collage, acrylic paint, stencils, ink drawing,
5 x 7 in. (12.7 x 17.8 cm)
Collection of Julie Selvagg

Basics

All objects are fair game

Creating fine art with found objects is no longer ridiculed by critics and the public as it was at the beginning of the twentieth century. Found objects as works of art—such as the urinal Marcel Duchamp signed and exhibited in 1917— are no longer shocking. Altered or not, we display all kinds of found objects—primitive stools, tools, or signs—as art in our homes, lit with spotlights or placed on pedestals.

Robert Rauschenberg's famous paintings of the early 1960s combined traditional canvases with paint-spattered antique quilts and taxidermied animals. They may not be to everyone's taste, but they're widely recognized as masterpieces of modern art. The visual language he and other Pop artists created has become an integral part of our culture.

Found objects speak to us all in one way or another. We're drawn to them because we assign personal meaning to them. They may remind us of other times and places, our youth, or a state of mind. And because we are naturally acquistive, we amass found objects in quantities

TERRY TAYLOR, *Ho, Ho, Ho*, 2003
45 rpm record, vintage stickers,
rubber-stamped and metal letters,
7 in. (17.8 cm)
Collection of Joe Rhatigan
Photo by Steve Mann

both large and small. Just look around your living and work spaces if you don't believe it.

When found objects are altered—however minimally—they take on new meaning. Viewers may immediately grasp the new meaning or, like all works of art should, the altered objects may become food for thought for the viewer.

There's no limit to the objects that can be altered. You'll find objects to alter in secondhand shops, discount stores, or in your very own closet. Working with some materials—wood, metal, or fiber—may require that you learn new techniques, but most of the techniques you already know will serve you well.

JULIANA COLES, *War Bride*, 2002
Wedding shoe, fabric flowers, trim, jewelry, feathers; stapled, dipped in wax, 9½ x 5½ x 2½ in. (24.1 x 14 x 6.4 cm)
Photo by Pat Berrett

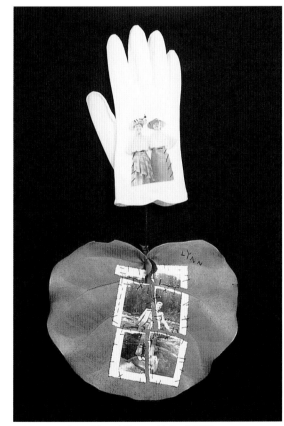

LYNN WHIPPLE, *Waxed Glove with Leaf*, 2003
Seagrape leaf, found images, handstiching, glove, beeswax, 6 x 13 x 1 in. (15.2 x 33 x 2.5 cm)
Photo by Randall Smith

HARRIETE ESTEL BERMAN, *Bittersweet Obsession*, 2003
Pre-printed steel from recycled tin containers, 10-karat gold, rivets, screws, resin, 20 x 15½ x 10¼ in. (50.8 x 39.4 x 26 cm)
Photo by Philip Cohen

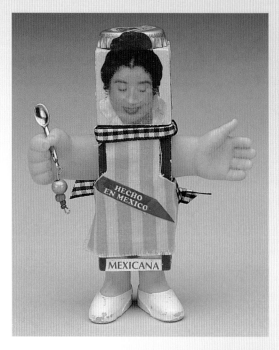

Clockwise from top left: *Artifact, Feed Your Soul, Plain Jane, Measure Up*

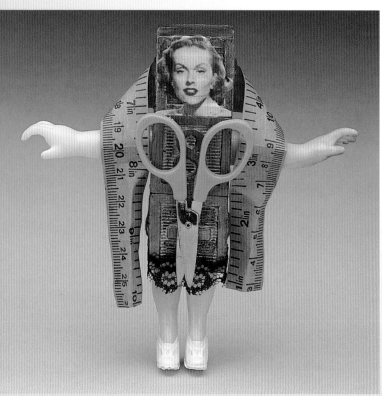

Blockheads

"There are so many possibilities for these fun little figures that creative block won't be a problem. Each blockhead has its own individual personality. A found piece of jewelry reminded me of a fish tail. The end, so to speak, was the beginning for the mermaid. The basic construction of each blockhead is similar. Your blockhead will have its own unique source of inspiration and personality."

Lina Trudeau Olson, DESIGNER

MATERIALS   Wooden blocks • Industrial strength adhesive • Doll parts • Acrylic gel medium • Acrylic paints • Embellishments • Small screw eyes • Small jump rings

1. Lina outlined the diameter of each leg and arm onto blocks, then used a drill to create shallow holes.

2. She fit the arms and legs in the holes and secured them with industrial strength adhesive.

3. Lina collaged and painted individual blocks for the torso and head of each doll. She finished each block with a coat of acrylic varnish to protect the collage elements.

4. After embellishing the blocks, Lina stacked the blocks and used industrial strength adhesive to attach them.

5. Lina attached small screw eyes to the tops and bottoms of the blocks to create a kinetic mermaid. She connected the screw eyes with small jump rings. To the head, she attached a single screw eye and threaded ribbon through it.

Fish Tales

Detail of *Artifact*

Altar-ed Tray

"There are many puns associated with the word tray. This game tray (for the bedridden?) was tres beau (very beautiful) and brought to mind the trey in dice and card games. The desire for good luck when throwing dice or any game of chance led to my creation of an altar with a triptych (there's that three again!)."

Bobby Hansson, DESIGNER

MATERIALS   Metal tray • Bottle caps • Metal stamps • Printed tins • Lucky horseshoe
Game pieces • Metal shears • Drill • Pop rivet tool and rivets

1. Bobby divided the tray into two unequal parts and cut it along a marked line with metal shears. He marked the shape for the triptych on the larger part and cut it out. The scrap pieces were set aside for later use.

2. He embossed the lettering on the tryptich with metal stamps. Then he folded in the side panels, using a strip of wood to keep the fold straight.

3. Bobby cut an image of Scrooge (counting his winnings?) from a candy tin. He used an industrial adhesive to apply the image to the metal.

4. He glued bottle caps to ceramic magnets to form a victory arch.

5. From the leftover tin scraps, he cut a printed shape and attached it to the triptych's point with a pop rivet. Then the triptych was riveted to the tray.

How to Pop Rivet

Your local home improvement store carries pop rivet tools and rivets of different lengths. If you like to work with metal, but don't want to or can't solder, a pop rivet tool is a handy tool to have.

• Punch or drill a hole in both pieces that you wish to join. Make the hole the same diameter as the stem of the pop rivet.

• Insert the rivet into the tool, and thread the rivet stem through the pieces you wish to join.

• Squeeze the handles of the tool. When the rivet pops, your pieces will be attached.

6. Bobby used another scrap of the leftover tin to create a candleholer. He cut out a simple cross shape, folded it to form a box, and riveted it together. He placed a horseshoe and supplicating hands on the altar. (Bobby insists that a supplicant, using secret ritual moves with the dice, tiddleywinks, jacks, and word cubes, will be given precious information. Powerball anyone?)

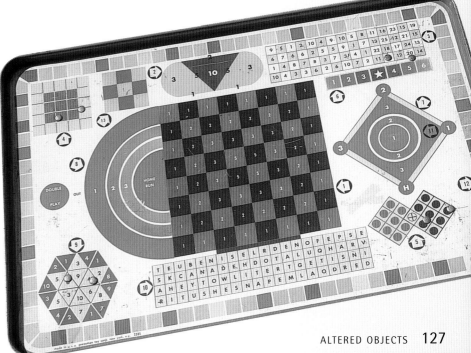

Photos by Bobby Hanson

I'll Fly Away

"I came across this vintage birdcage at a flea market and loved its shape. As I added pearls and gold, I began to think of women I knew as a child. These women valued beauty, harmony, formality, and manners above all else. As a child, I was in awe of their grace and polish. But as an adult, I recognize that there may have been times in their lives when they felt a bit trapped, held in place by their beautiful surroundings. I dedicate this piece to those women and to their unspoken moments, dreaming of another life."

Betsy Reeves, DESIGNER

MATERIALS   Birdcage • Spray paint • Acrylic paints • Faux pearls • Paper mache dress form
Feathers • Small box • Lamp finial • Decorative tissue paper • Rubber stamp • Stamping ink
Sealing wax • Raffia

1. Betsy disassembled the cage and sprayed it and its hardware with gold paint. After the paint dried, she glued pearls to the ridges of the roof.

2. She painted the dress form with acrylic paints, then added collaged and rubber-stamp images to the form.

3. Betsy loosely wrapped the form with raffia and added feather hanks glued to the shoulders for wings.

4. She melted sealing wax and poured it onto a heat-resistant surface. Before the wax completely cooled, Betsy pressed an inked rubber stamp into the wax. Then she glued the wax stamp to the torso.

5. Betsy covered the small box with tissue and glued the torso to it. Then she glued the assembly to the floor of the cage.

6. She arranged tissue paper around the base of the torso.

7. Betsy attached the finial to the roof with a screw and reassembled the cage.

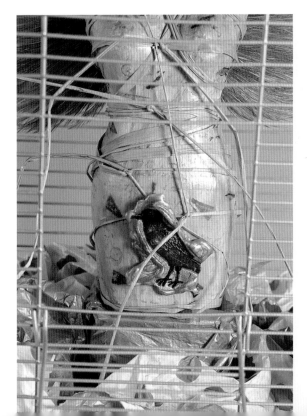

Altered Vest

"Elements from nature always seem to end up in my designs. This time I was thinking about my training as a pharmacist. Many of the medications we use today are derived from plants found around the world. The search continues for new sources of healing botanicals. This led me to think about a botanist who would wear this vest, traveling to faraway lands collecting specimens and having grand adventures."

Lynn B. Krucke, DESIGNER

MATERIALS

Vest • Fabric paints • Masking tape • Ink pads • Tags • Rubber stamps • Stickers • Sea glass Wire • Flat-backed floral marbles • Pressed leaves and petals • Slide mounts • Acetate • Brads Copper tooling foil • Metal alphabet stamp set • Metal eyelet alphabet • Plastic lizard

1. Lynn tore strips of masking tape in half and used the strips to mask off areas on the vest. Then she applied several colors of fabric paint, blending them before they dried.

2. After the paint dried, she used a permanent black ink to stamp images on the vest.

3. She aged shipping tags with dye inks and transferred additional images onto the tags. She slipped dried and silk leaves between two pieces of thin acetate, mounted them in slide mounts, and attached them to the vest with brads. She glued clear, flat-backed marbles on top of selected images and bits of plant material to magnify them.

4. Lynn cleverly replaced the vest's buttons with pieces of sea glass wrapped with wire. She tucked bundles of twigs, an aged map, and of course, a plastic lizard into the pockets.

5. She attached embossed metal plant labels to small plastic bags holding dried herbs and flowers.

How to Create Metal Labels

- Cut copper tooling foil into small strips.
- Use metal stamps to emboss the lettering on the metal.
- Heat the metal strips to create color on the labels. Hold a metal strip with long tweezers or a hemostat and heat the metal with a heat gun or by holding the metal over an open flame. Heat the copper until it changes colors.

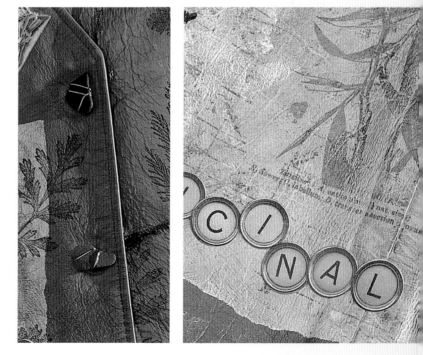

Sea glass buttons

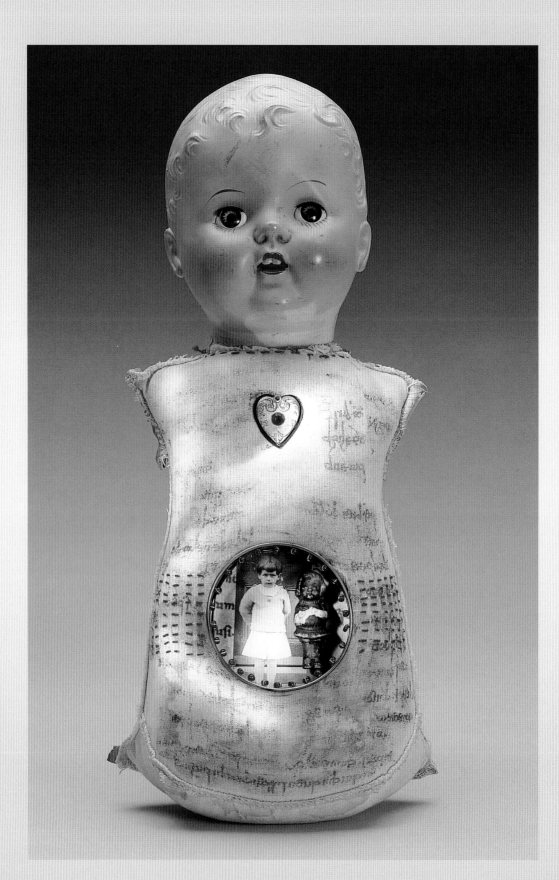

Altered Doll

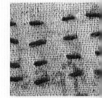

"I decided to give a vintage doll in less than perfect shape both new life and meaning. The unreadable text on the doll is like mysterious words or lessons from our past that are always with us. Tucked inside the tin are memories—like the ones we cherish of our own—and the mementos of childhood."

Nicole Tuggle, DESIGNER

MATERIALS   Cloth body doll • Image transfer • Tin box • Miniature toy • Beads
Charms • Embroidery thread

1. Nicole photocopied text from a vintage German book on handwriting analysis. Using a water slide transfer for silk material, she transferred the text onto the cloth body of the doll.

2. She traced the shape of the tin box onto the body.

3. Nicole pierced the rim of the tin with an awl to create small, evenly spaced holes. Then she stitched tiny beads in place with thread along the inside of the rim.

4. She created a collage to place inside the tin with a photocopy of a vintage photograph and her own handwritten text. She secured the small china doll to the collage with hot glue.

5. Nicole cut the body fabric approximately ¼ inch (6 mm) inside the line she marked in step 2. She added lines of simple running stitches, fit the tin snugly in the opening and secured it in place with glue.

Designer Tip

Here's an alternative way to secure the tin to the body. Don't stitch the beads to the tin, as described in step 3. Instead, stitch the tin to the cloth body. Slip a bead on your thread before you make each stitch.

6. Onto a slightly larger piece of black paper, Nicole glued a metal heart shape and embellished it with a solitary red faux jewel. She glued the entire assembly to the torso.

Trip to Santa Fe Journal Skirt

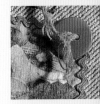

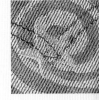

"My journal skirts, made from altered Levi's and Wranglers, are great fun to make and even more fun to wear—you get to stop and talk to people about them everywhere you go. This skirt documents a trip to Santa Fe, in June of 1998. It was our anniversary, and we had a terrific time. Journal skirts (and other journal clothing) are terrific for documenting trips and all sorts of other exciting adventures."

Ricë Freeman–Zachery, DESIGNER

MATERIALS • Skirt • Cotton fabric • Heat transfers • Rubber stamps • Fabric paint • Permanent fabric pens • Embroidery thread • Beads • Fabric trims

1. Ricë printed images on heat transfer paper. She transferred the images onto white cotton fabric, roughly trimmed them, and pinned them in place on the skirt.

Designer Tip

If you want a less crisp and softer image, transfer the image directly onto the garment fabric.

2. Ricë stamped titles and large text onto the skirt material with fabric paint. She created original hand-carved rubber stamps to stamp the zia symbol, red hot chiles, and larger letters (see page 50).

3. With permanent fabric marking pens, Ricë transcribed her personal journal entries onto the skirt.

4. She heat-set the inked and painted texts with an iron, following the manufacturer's recommendations.

Designer Tip

Heat-setting each and every piece of text takes a long time, but it's worth it. If you don't heat-set the garment, all of your hard work could disappear the first time you toss the skirt in the washing machine.

5. Ricë stitched the image transfers onto the skirt. She added fabric trims, embroidery, and beads to further embellish the skirt.

Left: Hand-carved rubber stamp imagery with embroidery
Below: Photo transfer directly on skirt fabric

Gallery

CHRIS GIFFIN, *Table Clock*, 2002
Antique tin, brass gears, vintage dial, vintage game
pieces, doll eyes, fishing lure; cold construction,
13½ x 6 x 4 in. (34.3 x 15.2 x 10.2 cm)
Photo by Ron Sawyer

DAYLE DOROSHOW, *Circle Puppets*, 2003
Wood blocks, polymer clay, color clay shading, photo transfer,
beads, 12 x 4 x 4 in. (30.5 x 10.2 x 10.2 cm)
Photos by Don Felton

MAGGIE YOWELL HALL, *Sacred Earth*, 2001
Globe, paper, acrylic paint; collaged, no dimensions
Photo by Julie Sotomura

*I created this collaged globe shortly after
September 11, 2001. All of the water bodies are
covered with sacred texts in different languages,
with passages about the earth, creation, war, and
peace. Tracing the exact outline of the land and
water with paper took several weeks.*

JUDITH HOYT

Black Pants, 2001
Found metal, wood, oil paint,
45 x 23½ x ¾ in. (114.3 x 59.7 x 1.9 cm)
Photo by John Lenz

Head with Green Lips, 2003
Found metal, wood, oil paint,
23¾ x 12 x ¾ in. (60.3 x 30.5 x 1.9 cm)
Photo by John Lenz

RUTH DANIELS, *Watermelon #1*, 2001
Found metals, acrylic paint, epoxy, 5⅛ x 10⅜ x 2 in. (12.7 x 26.4 x 5 cm)

LORI GREENE, *Metamorphosis*, 2003
Baby doll, superhero doll, stained glass beads, mosaic tile,
18 x 15 x 10 in. (45.7 x 38.1 x 25.4 cm)
Photo by artist

MICHAEL STASIUK, *Lobster Marionette*, 2002
Boxing gloves, baseball shin guard, football shoulder pads, hockey
stick, game pieces, 39 x 50 x 6 in. (99 x 127 x 15.2 cm)
Courtesy of Clark Gallery
Photo by Andrew Edgar

The tail—a baseball shin guard—was the starting point.
I saw the lobster at that point and said, "Wouldn't it be
amazing if I could find the rest of the lobster?" It took
two years but I did eventually find the rest.

DONNA ROSENTHAL, *Button Ladies: Past Life Quilt*, 1998
Vintage damask table linen, vintage buttons; embroidered,
18 x 19 x 1 in. (45.7 x 48.3 x 2.5 cm)
Courtesy of Bernice Steinbaum Gallery, Miami, Florida, U.S.
Photo by Adam Reich

I observe, question and examine the nature of relationships—how personal
perceptions and romantic interactions have been eternally influenced by
society and culture. As I gather and recount stories and rituals, I explore the
connection between historical and societal pressures and our thoughts and
reactions, clearly the subject of art, craft, music, literature, games, and toys. In
my work, I use text, repetition, and the cultural symbolism of clothing to
expose the resulting struggles between the external and internal self. The
manner in which I compose my work and each element of the work–materials,
images, content and process–are carefully planned to give clues to the personal
and collective realities of our longings, presumptions, and predicaments.

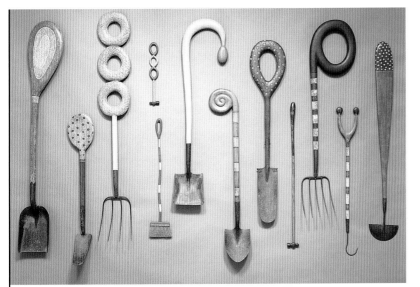

ANDY BUCK, *Rehandled Tools*, 1999
Found implements, wood; carved, painted, various dimensions
Collection of Peter Joseph Estate
Photo by Phil Harris

HARRIETE ESTEL BERMAN, *Material Identity*, 2001
Pre-printed steel from recycled tin containers, aluminum, sterling silver, 10-karat gold rivets, screws, 38¼ x 17¼ x 14 in. (97.2 x 43.8 x 35.6 cm)
Photo by Philip Cohen

DAYLE DOROSHOW, *The Wishing Chair*, 2002
Wood chair, polymer clay, patina, photo transfers, gold leaf; carved, 11 x 4 x 4 in. (27.9 x 10.2 x 10.2 cm)
Photo by Don Felton

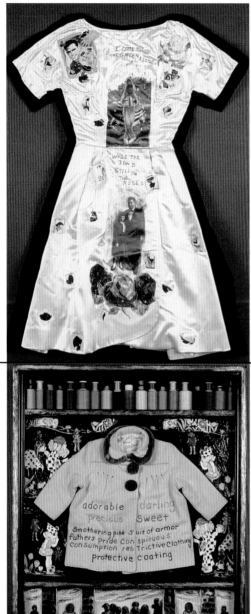

CHRIS GIFFIN, *Equine Journey Neckpiece*, 2003
Vintage tins, milagros, metal numbers, erector set
pieces, metal tape measure; cold construction,
4⅛ x 3 x ¼ in. (10.2 x 7.6 x .6 cm)
Photo by Ron Sawyer

MADONNA C. PHILLIPS

Father's Day Sunday Dress, 2001
Dress, mixed media
Photo by Cheryl Gottschall

Protective Coating, 2003
Child's coat, mixed media
30 x 3 x 40 in. (76.2 x 7.6 x 101.6 cm)
Photo by Cheryl Gottschall

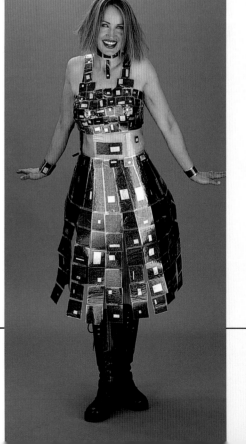

DEE FONTANS, *Wearable Edibles/Nori Dress*, 2003
Nori, 24-karat gold, plastic, tape; laminated, taped,
43 x 22 x 22 in. (109.2 x 55.8 x 55.8 cm)
Modeled by Mona Dallmann
Photo by Stu Swamp

ACKNOWLEDGMENTS

Many thanks to the 95 artists from around the country who responded to the call for gallery images.

Kudos to Rebecca Guthrie (and her pal, Sybil) for their crack organizational skills and kind forbearance.

9 Ah, thank you for your lending your keen eye, kind words, and regaling me with raucous laughter. Not necessarily in that order.

Here is the last thing you need to lay out this book, Ms. Pfeffer. Thank you very much for your patience and graphic élan.

TERRY TAYLOR, *Oraculum*, 1999
Found objects, 5½ x 12 in. (14 cm x 30.5 cm)
Photo by Robert Chiarito

DESIGNERS

Nina Bagley lives in Sylva, North Carolina, with her two sons, Robin and Roy, and her springer spaniel, Aspen. For 17 years her full-time career has been transforming vintage images, natural materials, and words into sterling silver collage jewelry. Her list of publications includes *Somerset Studio Magazine*, *The Decorated Page* (Lark, 2002), *Collage for the Soul* (Rockport, 2003), and *True Colors: A Palette of Collaborative Art Journals* (Somerset Studio Publishers, 2003). Visit Nina's website at www.itsmysite.com/ninabagleydesign/.

Ricë Freeman-Zachery is an artist and author living in Midland, Texas. She's the author of *Stamp Artistry* (Rockport, 2003) and numerous articles in *Art Doll Quarterly*, *Belle Armoire*, and *Somerset Studio*. Her artwear, dolls, and jewelry can be found in shops and galleries from the French Quarter in New Orleans to Canyon Road in Santa Fe.

Suzanne Gernandt is a fiber artist who lives and works in Asheville, North Carolina. She's a member of the Southern Highland Craft Guild and has taught at Penland School of Crafts.

Bobby Hansson is a well-known craftsman, photographer, teacher, and the author of *The Fine Art of the Tin Can* (Lark, 1996). His sartorial élan is legendary in certain circles, as he combines three (or more!) plaids into one stunning ensemble. He lives in Rising Sun, Maryland.

Megan Kirby is an art director at Lark Books, as well as an occasional project designer. She lives in Asheville, North Carolina, where she enjoys working on her house and garden while her cat, Elliot watches.

Lynne Krucke lives in Summerville, South Carolina. She's a versatile designer and workshop instructor in many media—polymer clay, beading, rubber-stamping, and precious metal clay. Contact her at lkrucke@bellsouth.net.

Jane LaFerla is an editor at Lark Books. She recently "retired" from her part-time job as co-owner of Gallery of the Mountains in Asheville, North Carolina. So now, in her spare time, she's working on a novel.

Barbara Matthiessen is a mixed-media artist and teacher who resides in the Pacific Northwest with her husband and darling dog, Coltrane. She's the author of *New Metal Foil Crafts* (Rockport, 2002) and co-author of *Collage Creations* (North Light, 2004).

Susan McBride is an artist who has worked in the field of graphic design for the last 20 years. She alleges she was born with a crayon in her hand and has sketched or painted all of her life. In her workaday life, she's an art director at Lark Books. She lives in Asheville, North Carolina, with her family, two cats, and a dog.

Katie Metheny is an occupational therapist in Asheville, North Carolina. When she isn't providing therapy to patients, she likes to work with fibers, collage, and printing.

Jean Tomaso Moore is a mixed-media artist who has created projects for several Lark books. Her goal in life is to be as prolific an artist as Terry Taylor, but she realizes she will probably need another lifetime to catch up. Jean lives in Asheville, North Carolina, with her funky, guitarist husband, Richard. Contact her at LeaningTowerArt@MSN.COM.

Lina Trudeau Olson is an elementary art educator in Asheville, North Carolina. Her time is balanced between the classroom, the studio, and her young family. She finds this lively mix to be a constant source of inspiration and enthusiasm.

Sheila Longo Petruccelli lives in an old farmhouse in Alexander, North Carolina, with her hilarious husband and cherubic son. She enjoys making art with vintage items and things that would otherwise wind up in the landfill. You can email her at slpetruccelli@charter.net.

Jane Powell left the hustle and bustle of city life (and mortgage banking!) in Chicago in 1994 to move to the quiet mountain town of Saluda, North Carolina. Her shop on Saluda's thriving Main Street—The Stamp Peddler—offers an intriguing array of paper, rubber stamps, and needful supplies for artists and crafters. Visit her website at www.stamppeddler.com.

Betsy Reeves lives and works in Asheville, North Carolina. She's been working with collage and assemblage for over ten years.

Jane Reeves is primarily known for her art quilts that have been included in *Quilt National* and other exhibitions. Her work is found in numerous corporate and private collections in the United States, Saudi Arabia, and Japan. She lives in Black Mountain, North Carolina.

Tracy Roos is a multimedia artist living and working in Portland, Oregon. Visit her website, www.tracyroos.com.

Valerie Shrader is an editor at Lark Books. Her page (page 67) was inspired by her grandmother, Polly Van Arsdale, who added love to everything she sewed, knit, smocked, appliqued, or embroidered.

Katherine Sullivan lives in Nashville, Tennessee. Her artwork has been published in *Somerset Studio*, *Belle Armoire*, and *Expression* magazines.

Jen Swearington's mixed-media quilts and paintings have been exhibited around the country. Most recently, one of her quilts was included in the Dairy Barn's touring exhibit *Quilt National 2003*. She lives in Asheville, North Carolina, where she teaches part-time and operates Jennythreads Studio. Visit her website at www.jennythreads.net.

Terry Taylor is the author or co-author of eight Lark books. When he's not working on books or projects for Lark Books, he's a mixed-media artist and jeweler. He has studied jewelry and metal work at John C. Campbell Folk School, Appalachian Center for Crafts, and Haystack Mountain School of Crafts.

Nicole Tuggle is an artist with a background in drawing, correspondence art, and collage. Her assemblage constructions and illustrations reflect a passion for salvaging the found object. View more of her work at www.sigilation.com.

Luann Udell is the author of *The Weekend Crafter: Rubber Stamp Carving* (Lark, 2002). She's a talented designer and mixed-media artist whose work is inspired by prehistoric art and artifacts. Visit her website at www.durable-goods.com.

Lynn Whipple's whimsical work is shown nationally in juried exhibitions and in galleries. Her work has been published in books and national magazines. She shares a warehouse studio in Winter Park, Florida, with her husband, John, and twenty-four other artists who she thinks of as her extended family. At the moment, she is the reigning queen of the ongoing foosball championships at McRae Art Studios.

Jane Ann Wynn creates mixed-media works in Parkville, Maryland. Her works are shown in galleries in Maryland, Washington D.C., and internationally. She displays her works online at www.wynnstudio.com.

Chris Young is a self-taught artist from St. Louis, Missouri. She's an administrative coordinator at Washington University while working toward a degree in psychology. Her card designs have been published in *Rubberstamper* and *Stampers' Sampler* magazines.

CONTRIBUTING GALLERY ARTISTS

Carole Austin, Orinda, California (96)

Harriete Estel Berman, San Mateo, California (123,139)

Joseph Borzotta, New York, New York (95)

Andy Buck, Honeoye Falls, New York (139)

Juliana Coles, Albuquerque, New Mexico (76, 123)

Patricia Chapman, Santa Fe, New Mexico (78, 94)

Ruth Daniels, Somerville, Massachusetts (137)

Dayle Doroshaw, Ft. Bragg, California (Title page, 32, 136, 139)

Dorit Elisha, Sunnyvale, California (35, 79)

Dee Fontans, Calgary, Alberta, Canada (140)

Lisa Glicksman, Oakland, California (120)

Lori Greene, St. Paul, Minnesota (137)

Chris Giffin, Mount Vernon, Washington, (136, 140)

Maggie Yowell Hall, Seattle, Washington (136)

Deborah Hayner, San Francisco, California (82, 83, 97)

Claudine Hellmuth, Orlando, Florida (14, 121)

Judith Hoyt, New Paltz, New York (Title page, 137)

Shari Kadison, Boston, Massachusetts (97)

Gwendolyn McLarty, Houston, Texas (120)

Katie Metheny, Asheville, North Carolina (37)

Carol Owen, Pittsboro, North Carolina (41, 77)

Madonna Phillips, Raleigh, North Carolina (Title page, 140)

Roxene Rockwell, Los Angeles, California (21)

Donna Rosenthal, New York, New York (138)

Ron Sawyer, Mount Vernon, Washington (97)

Dawn Southworth, Gloucester, Massachusetts (121)

Michael Stasiuk, Portsmouth, New Hampshire (138)

Mary Tafoya, Albuquerque, New Mexico (95)

Nicole Tuggle, Asheville, North Carolina (95)

Judy Watt, San Francisco, California (79)

Lynne Whipple, Winter Park, Florida (Title page, 83, 123)

Jaye Whitworth, Long Beach, California (78)

Dawn Wilson, South Grafton, Massachusetts (76)

Index